The New
Winsome
Witnessing

Dynamic Ways to Share Your Faith

by Gary Gibbs

Dedicated to the memory of Elder O. J. Mills and
to his dear wife, Millie—models of *Winsome Witnessing*.

Distributed by
Seminars Unlimited
PO Box 66
Keene, TX 76059
(817) 641-3643

Original title *Winsome Witnessing, Dynamic Ways to Share Your Faith*
First Printing 2003
Second Printing 2004
Third Printing, Revised and Expanded 2011

Cover Design by Haley Trimmer
Cover Art by goodsalt.com
Text Design by Greg Solie • AltamontGraphics.com

ISBN: 978-0-9728217-0-4

CONTENTS

4

FOREWORD

Most people do not have as much apprehension in coming to Jesus as they do attempting to share Him in a secular age and culture. Many are even terrified with the thought of sharing their faith with their friends and family. Yet it is a crucial part of the experience for any spiritually healthy Christian. The only way a believer can have a vibrant faith is if they are giving their faith away.

What would you give to see your loved ones in heaven? Spotting their smiling, radiant faces in the throng standing on the golden pavement and basking in the dazzling beams of God's magnificent presence? Isn't that more valuable to us than anything else? If this is life's ultimate priority, allow me to pose a question: How will the people we love get to heaven? We know Jesus is the only entrance pass to its wonderland of bliss. But before a person can give their life to the Saviour, they must first hear about Him. So who is going to tell them? This is where we come in. *Witnesses.* That's what God calls us. We are the spark plug that ignites their launch to paradise.

Perhaps like me, you have had opportunities to witness but didn't know what to say? Many times we would rather say nothing than the wrong thing. Frozen by fear, we allow ourselves to become spiritual mutes in an effort not to prejudice others. The devil has mired millions of professed Christians in the swamp of imaginary fears. We don't have to be immobilized by doubts any longer.

This inspiring book you hold in your hands will help to melt the ice that paralyzes many believers and infuse the reader with peace, confidence, and practical instruction in how to share their faith and be a *"Winsome Witness."*

As friends and associates, at home and around the world, Gary Gibbs and I have worked together in soul winning for many years. I have learned much from his thoughtful understanding of the biblical science of personal evangelism. He has proven these principles in the laboratory of experience as a teacher, evangelist, and witness for the Master. Read this and watch your harvest of souls multiply as your joy and enthusiasm explodes!

Doug Batchelor,
President, *Amazing Facts*

PREFACE
TO THE NEW WINSOME WITNESSING

When I first began sharing my faith as a new Christian, I soon learned that to be effective I had to be trained. God provided this through godly mentors such as Elder O.J. and Millie Mills, Joe Crews, and others who have had a lasting impact on my ministry. He also gave me real-life experiences going into homes to present Bible studies and preaching evangelistic meetings. Making my own mistakes, sensing the Spirit's impressions, and seeing positive results are among the greatest teachers I've known.

This book is a synthesis of my many years learning best how to win others to Jesus. Those who read the original *Winsome Witnessing* tell me it was not only fun to read and extremely practical, but it has helped them win souls. God has used *Winsome Witnessing* in ways far beyond my expectations. More than 40,000 copies are in print. It has been translated into multiple languages including Portuguese, Romanian, German, Russian, and others. Students in evangelism training schools around the world, pastors, evangelists, and lay people have told me how they have benefitted and used these principles to help others embrace salvation.

While the original *Winsome Witnessing* has produced amazing results, I am especially excited about this expanded edition, *The New Winsome Witnessing*. For many years, I have wanted to include chapters on the vital topic of how to disciple new converts. I have also desired to expand certain areas to help readers be even more effective. This new version includes this and much more!

In addition, you are receiving my popular *Winsome Studies in Prophecy* book on CD-ROM. This book contains the actual presentation notes that I use to give a Bible study. These notes form a large part of my success and are being used by others with similar results. With these in hand you will have the confidence to present Bible prophecy in a clear, convincing way. In fact, even recently baptized members frequently tell me how *Winsome Studies in Prophecy* makes it easy for them to immediately give prophetic studies to their family and friends. It is that simple.

When you use these presentation scripts along with my *Prophecies of Hope* lessons (sold separately), you will see your Bible students stay engaged and make decisions for Christ. (You present the Bible study by using the *Winsome Studies* notes. After the study you leave with your student the corresponding *Prophecies of Hope* lesson for them to study on their own. This is explained in more detail in both books.) The *Prophecies of Hope* study guides were especially written to help you succeed in real-world soul-winning. I have included proven phrases and techniques to help your students relax, learn, and open their hearts to Bible truth. One very helpful feature of the *Prophecies of Hope* lessons is that they make the truth so obvious that they neutralize and bypass the objections people typically give. I believe that once you try the *Winsome Studies* and *Prophecies of Hope* lessons, you will discover that your students possess a convicting understanding of the relevance of the Sabbath and other doctrines. This will translate into helping you build stronger relationships and seeing more baptismal decisions.

My purpose in writing *The New Winsome Witnessing*, *Winsome Studies in Prophecy*, and *Prophecies of Hope* series is to help God's people in all walks of life successfully share their faith and hasten Jesus' return. It is my prayer that by obtaining these three resources, you will be inspired, trained, and equipped to experience God using you with fresh power and new success.

To further advance your training, I also invite you to visit the church growth training website I started, www.HopeNETonline.org. There you will find even more free evangelism training resources and videos on virtually every aspect of church growth. You can use these videos for your own training or to host training events at your church.

May God richly bless you to be His winsome witness!

Gary Gibbs

Chapter 1
TAMING YOUR NERVES

A fearful realization engulfed me as I stood on the corner looking at the long row of houses stretching down the street. I didn't have a clue as to what to say at the first door! As a baby Christian, I was convicted to sell Christian books. Here I was on my first day on the job with my product in hand. What was I supposed to do now? What if they had questions I couldn't answer? What if they didn't want me there? A thousand "what ifs" tortured my mind. I sat on that street corner for over two hours before I settled my nerves enough to knock on the first door. The experience lurking there confirmed all my anxieties. They treated me like I was a poor refugee trying to move into their neighborhood. So I went to the next door. There I found the same depressing "un" welcome. Door after door slammed in my face. I couldn't even *give* the books away. As one elderly lady made her quick retreat inside, she swept my free book aside knocking it to the ground. Before I even made it half way down the street I decided to go home.

But I didn't give up. I found a friend who used to sell books. The next week I gave it another try this time with John's reinforcement at my side. He worked really hard to impress me. At the first home an innocent enough looking man opened the door wide. John introduced us, *"Hi, my name is John and this is Gary. We are visiting people in the neighborhood and showing them ways to prevent juvenile delinquency. May we come in?"* Without a moment's hesitation, John quickly ducked past the unsuspecting chap, sprinted over to his living room sofa and promptly sat down with a big grin on his face. He had shown me how to get in. Fortunately for us, the shocked victim of our home invasion looked at me and with resignation said, *"Well, I guess you might as well come in too."* While I didn't adopt all the clever practices I learned that day, I did discover ways to visit in homes. And this led to one of the most exciting discoveries of my early Christian experience. There are people all around us looking and praying for God to send someone to teach them His truth.

On my very first day as a Bible instructor, I drove up to an apartment complex to visit Peggy. I had a card indicating she had received *Signs* magazine at one time. Since the apartments were not numbered I had to ask a man working on his car if he knew where Peggy lived. It turned out the shade tree mechanic, David, was her husband. We went into their home and I told them I had some fascinating Bible studies that might interest them. David acted absolutely astonished. He told me he had recently given his heart to God. For months he painstakingly visited church after church looking for one that truly followed the Bible. That very Sunday he gave up on his elusive search. He told God, *"I can't find your church. If you want to lead me to your people you're going to have to send them to me."* Bang! Just like that I was there the next day. David and Peggy turned out to be excellent Bible students with many questions. At the end of our studies together they both were baptized.

The very word *witnessing* strikes terror in the hearts of believers and non-believers alike. Mention it in a crowd of Christians and they freeze up. They get a look I've seen in the face of possums caught in my headlights on a dark country road. Possums are ugly enough in the bright daylight. Worse still, any time of day, is the look on the face of a terrified Christian cornered by the personal ministries leader on outreach Sabbath. It's not a pretty sight. Feelings of inadequacy, lack of knowledge, fear of failure and a host of negative thoughts paralyze them. Most succumb to these demons of doubt instead of conquering them. But faith can sweep fear aside and free us to feel the Spirit of God flowing into our lives, enabling us to do things we only dreamt about. Perhaps the reason we don't experience more of God's power is because we live too safely. What would happen if we ventured out of our comfort zones and trusted God?

Some friends and I once gave Bible studies to Bob. I was new at this and had only a few feeble lessons prepared in advance. After a couple of studies, God began to change Bob's heart. His fellow employees noticed he was more patient and questioned him about it. One co-worker was especially interested. Bob began sharing our studies with him. Bob received a new study one week from us and the following week he presented it to his co-worker. Bob was never more than one simple study ahead of *his* student. When the day arrived for Bob's baptism, he had the heavenly joy of knowing that in the neighboring town, his co-worker was also being baptized.

The number one fear of witnessing that grips many is the feeling that their Bible knowledge is only at the kindergarten level. They feel unprepared unless that knowledge is at a Ph.D. level. If this is your concern, remember Bob. To lead someone else to Jesus you only need to be one baby step ahead of them. You certainly don't need to be able to recite the entire Hebrew and Greek text. When was the last time that you heard a truly interesting sermon using that stuff anyway? It is enough to begin with the little information you do possess.

Too many are waiting for a wealth of knowledge they will never realize until they go out and share the pittance they have. "He who begins with a *little knowledge*, in a humble way, and *tells what he knows*, while seeking diligently for further knowledge, will find the whole heavenly treasure awaiting his demand. *The more he seeks to impart light, the more light he will receive.* The more one *tries* to explain the Word of God to others, with a love for souls, *the plainer it becomes to himself.* The more we use our knowledge and exercise our powers, the more knowledge and power we shall have" (*Christ's Object Lessons*, p. 354; all emphasis supplied unless otherwise noted).

This is a powerful promise! The key to getting more knowledge is to give away what you have. The little lad with two fish and five barley loaves gave all he had to Jesus and found himself sitting ringside at the greatest show on earth. What if he had rationalized that his food was much too small to take care of the hungry masses? Many would have missed the blessing of a mammoth miracle. I wonder how many miracles we miss because we listen to our fears.

There is nothing better calculated to teach us the truth than for us to instruct someone else. As I witness to people and give studies, God gives me insights and makes truth clearer to my own mind than at any other time. There are occasions when the new ideas are so compelling, I actually take notes so I won't forget the points. If you want to know your Bible and feel the joy of being used by God, don't give in to Satan's nagging temptation to look at your own inadequacy. Allow faith to tame your jittery nerves and then step back to watch God work exciting miracles in your life as you become a "winsome witness."

Discuss, Learn, Apply

1. List several fears that keep many Christians from sharing their faith.

2. What is your biggest fear, or thing, that may keep you from witnessing?

3. Read again Ellen White's statement on *Christ Object Lessons*, page 354. What do these words say to you personally?

4. How do you feel about sharing your faith?

Chapter 2
WINNING 'EM WITHOUT KILLING 'EM

*L*et me give you an embarrassing example of how *not* to witness. Before I share this story I must confess that most of what I know about winsome witnessing I've learned by making more mistakes than I care to admit. One of my early blunders happened so close to my own baptism that I doubt my hair had even dried. I was seventeen-years-old and still living at home. My mother had recently married Ben, who turned out to be an alcoholic and one who was very antagonistic to my new faith.

With the enthusiasm of a galloping herd of buffalo, I decided to witness to my needy stepfather. I figured he was so hard-headed that I needed to hit him with the big guns. I earnestly informed him that the head of *his* church was the antichrist himself. Talk about a lack of tact. For some strange reason, Ben wasn't buying it. *"Well,"* I calculated, *"some people will decide for Christ only as the last grains of sand are slipping through the hourglass of probation."* I would have to give him an unmistakable sign that would one day prove me right and convince him to believe as I did. So, irrespective of my faulty theology and pig-headed methods, I told him that in the last days, the antichrist would call a lightning bolt of blazing fire down out of heaven to prove he was God's legitimate leader. I solemnly warned Ben he must not be deceived.

Ben listened with a rapt attention that I later learned was utter shock. His response, though, made me realize I had not gotten through to him. *"If I see a man call fire down from heaven, I will go up and shake his hand and tell him he is a man of God!"*

I thought right then I had enough evidence to convince a grand jury that this man was unredeemable. He was impossible! And I told him so. Before the smoke cleared, he and I were nose-to-nose shouting at each other. (I'm thankful that my character in those days is a thing of the past.) The heated argument became so white hot that in my desire to save Ben's soul we threatened to kill each other. Here I was only trying to save him, but in my immature zeal I was going to drag his still warm corpse to Jesus as my trophy for sharing God's truth.

My mother pried us apart and I stormed off to my room. There God spoke to my heart. He told me that I was to apologize with no "ifs, ands or buts." I really wrestled with God over this. I figured if Ben had not been so obstinate I wouldn't have needed to say what I did. Thankfully, the Lord quieted my groveling excuses. I offered Ben a sincere, honest and heartfelt apology. It was probably as difficult for him to receive the apology as it was for me to give it, but both of us found a peace and new relationship that was gratifying. Later when he was confronted with the difficult decision to be treated for alcoholism, I was the only one in his family that he listened to.

Relationships are essential to change lives. As a young Christian I thought everyone would appreciate the truth I proclaimed. Was I ever wrong. The poor results I experienced eloquently testified that I was aiming my gospel ammo at the wrong target. Many make the same miserable mistake. One eager new evangelist told me he thought that all he needed for success was to advertise that he was teaching the Bible. He fully expected people to clamor to get into the meeting hall and baptistery. He was extremely disappointed with the paltry results of his intellectually-based sermons.

This is a common error of most novice soul winners. We aim to convince the intellect and conscience, but fail to reach the heart. The heart is the seat of emotion. It is the place where most people make life-changing decisions. While we must educate the mind and conscience with eternal truth, we also need to appeal to the heart to inspire conviction and decision. "When truth is held as truth only by the conscience, when the heart is not stimulated and made receptive, only the mind is affected. But when the truth is received as truth by the heart, it has passed through the conscience, and has captivated the soul with its pure principles. It is placed in the heart by the Holy Spirit, who reveals its beauty to the mind, that its transforming power may be seen in the character" (*Evangelism*, p. 291).

Winsome witnessing is much more than simply telling someone that Jesus is coming soon. There are people who think they fulfill the Great Commission by emblazoning the truth of the seventh-day Sabbath and the identity of the antichrist on billboards and in newspapers around the world.

Hitting people over the head with Bible texts is probably the worse witness we can have. During the Reformation a group of fervent Protestants were determined to get the truth out to everyone. "Placards attacking the mass were in one night posted all over France. Instead of advancing the reform, this zealous but ill-judged movement brought ruin, not only upon its propagators, but upon the friends of the reformed faith throughout France. It gave the Romanists what they had long desired—a pretext for demanding the utter destruction of the heretics as agitators dangerous to the stability of the throne and the peace of the nation" (*The Great Controversy*, p. 224, 225).

I am afraid we fall into a trap when we think the public evangelist's manner of forceful preaching is the model we should imitate in our personal witnessing. What most people fail to recognize is that evangelists develop relationships that win them the right to share the truth. Evangelists preach like a lion, but they make personal visits like a lamb.

The reason we are not more successful in our outreach efforts is because we neglect to build relationships. It was when I spoke to Ben's heart that I finally reached his head. There needs to be more emphasis placed on talking to a person's heart as we win them to Christ. We could help to better arm baby believers if we taught them this as they came out of the baptistery.

Several years after my failed attempt to witness I read the advice of a successful personal evangelist. I learned that we can be much more productive if we will find ways to reach people at the heart level. Here are some vital insights into winsome witnessing that we would do well to remember. As you read these illuminating statements please make note of the many practical ways we can utilize to reach hearts hungry for Christ.

"Your *success* will not depend so much upon your knowledge and accomplishments, as upon your ability to *find your way to the heart*. By being *social* and *coming close* to the people, you may turn the current of their thoughts more readily than by the most able discourse" (*Gospel Workers*, p. 193).

"While He ministered to the poor, Jesus *studied* also to find ways of reaching the rich. He *sought the acquaintance* of the wealthy and cultured Pharisee, the Jewish nobleman, and Roman ruler. He *accepted* their invitations, *attended* their feasts, made Himself *familiar* with their interests and occupations, *that he might gain access to their hearts*, and reveal to them the imperishable riches" (*The Ministry of Healing*, p. 24, 25).

"There is need of *coming close to the people* by personal effort. If less time were given to sermonizing, and more time were spent in *personal ministry, greater results* would be seen. The poor are to be relieved, the sick cared for, the sorrowing and bereaved comforted, the ignorant instructed, the inexperienced counseled. ... *Accompanied by the power of persuasion, the power of prayer, the power of the love of God, this work will not, cannot, be without fruit*" (*The Ministry of Healing*, p. 143, 144).

"*Go to your neighbors one by one*, and *come close* to them till their *hearts* are warmed by your unselfish interest and love. *Sympathize* with them, **pray** with them, *watch* for opportunities to *do them good*, and as you can, gather a few together and *open the Word* of God to their darkened minds" (*Review and Herald*, March 13, 1888).

Relationship building truly is the secret to successful witnessing. An evangelistic meeting is currently considered a victory when ten, twenty, or forty are baptized. If one hundred commit their lives to God we are ecstatic. But what would happen if the majority of our members served from hearts overflowing with God's love? This type of love accompanied by the power of persuasion and prayer will reap a bountiful harvest that will astound us. Here is a promise that assures us this is the case. "If we would humble ourselves before God, and be kind and courteous and tenderhearted and pitiful, there would be *one hundred conversions* to the truth where now there is *only one*" (*Testimonies for the Church*, Vol. 9, p. 189). Exponential growth awaits us!

STRATEGY FOR WINSOME WITNESSING

AUDIENCE: "Go to your neighbors one by one" (*Review and Herald*, March 13, 1888).

TARGET: "Find your way to the heart" (*Gospel Workers*, p. 193).

METHOD: "Coming close to the people" (*The Ministry of Healing*, p. 143).

MEANS: "Sympathize ... pray with them, watch for opportunities to do them good ... and open the Word of God" (*The Review and Herald*, March 13, 1888).

DON'T NEGLECT: "Power of persuasion, the power of prayer, the power of the love of God" (*The Ministry of Healing*, p. 144).

RESULTS: "One hundred conversions to the truth where now there is only one" (*Testimonies for the Church*, Vol. 9, p. 189).

Discuss, Learn, Apply

1. This chapter stresses the importance of relationships. What do these thoughts mean to you practically as you work to win people for Jesus?

2. What kind of mistakes do many Christians make when sharing their faith?

3. Read again Ellen White's counsel on the role of relationships in soul-winning and write down the points you find most relevant.

4. Describe how you can utilize the principles you've learned from this chapter in witnessing to a neighbor, co-worker, family, friend, or someone else. Write thier name and then a relationship building strategy that you can begin using.

Chapter 3
REMEDY FOR LAODICEA

I consider what happened to me one year after I became a Christian to be a major turning point in my life. Early one morning in the privacy of my room, I was reading Jesus' message to His last-day church in Revelation 3:14–22 when the Spirit of God burst into my conscience like a tank rolling through a wall. A powerful conviction seized me that without the ongoing intervention of God, my inevitable destiny was to be a lost Laodicean. I couldn't imagine a more awful fate. I dropped to my knees and sincerely begged God to do whatever it might take to keep me from this deadly self-deception.

Shortly afterwards God began steering me into situations where I could actively share Christ with others. I started by selling Christian literature and then moved into giving Bible studies. Today I am an evangelist and ordained pastor.

As I look back over more than three decades, I see many times where God used my witnessing activity to stoke the low-burning embers of my then flickering faith. If I was tempted with discouragement, I soon found myself in a home counseling a discouraged person with the very words I needed to hear. Frustrated with people in church? God led me to mend the broken spirit of someone who had given up on the saints. Tempted to just coast in my faith? I met a man whose life was shattered because he carelessly made irreversible decisions that permanently marred his happiness. Working for others has repeatedly been God's direct answer for my prayer of protection against Laodiceanism.

Even though full-time ministry is not God's goal for everyone, Christian service is His antidote for every Laodicean. "The best medicine you can give the church is not preaching or sermonizing, but planning work for them. If set to work, the despondent would soon forget their despondency, the weak would become strong, the ignorant intelligent, and all would be prepared to present the truth as it is in Jesus" (*Evangelism*, p. 356).

"As we seek to win others to Christ, bearing the burden of souls in our prayers, our own hearts will throb with the quickening influence of God's grace; our own affections will glow with more divine fervor; our whole Christian life will be more of a reality, more earnest, more prayerful" (*Christ's Object Lessons*, p. 354).

Are you spiritually dead? Then give studies. It will motivate you to pray more. Don't know your Bible? Give studies. You will dig into the Scriptures like never before. Is your church dry and uninviting? Get the members giving studies and watch the passion of their first love return. "God calls upon every church member to enter His service. Truth that is not *lived*, that is not *imparted to others*, loses its life-giving power, its healing virtue" (*Testimonies for the Church*, Vol. 8, p. 47, author's emphasis).

We live in a time when it is essential that we explain the Word of God to others. There are bewildered people all around us wandering aimlessly along the highway of life. Many of them will be hopelessly lost if we don't personally befriend, pray and labor for them. "Many have gone down to ruin who might have been saved if their neighbors, common men and women, had put forth personal effort for them. Many are waiting to be personally addressed. In the very family, the neighborhood, the town where we live, there is work for us to do as missionaries" (*The Desire of Ages*, p. 141).

Embracing this idea is like hugging a porcupine. We don't want this dropped in our laps! It feels safer to us to run in the footsteps of Jonah and try to convince ourselves that God understands that this is not *our* gift. Surely He is not *that* dependent on us and can find some other means to reach our neighbors.

While God will use a vast variety of ways to reach people, He wants to use *us*. It is the cumulative influence of numerous means that leads a person to come to Christ. Soul winners as great as the apostle Paul recognized this. He said, "I have planted, Apollos watered; but God gave the increase" (1 Corinthians 3:6).

Our part in another's salvation is more essential than we think. We may be the only person they'll ever encounter who has the personality and life experience to really connect with them. How many persons have you met who are close enough to you to significantly change your life? Like most, chances are you will answer that you can count intimate friends such as these on the fingers of one hand. It is the same way with the lost. How many people will they meet in their lifetime who know Christ and His truth and will make the effort to win them? Without our influence, all of the other elements God has placed in their path may add up to nothing. We are eternally significant.

There is also the issue of our own spirituality to consider. Christians who do not carry the gospel to others cripple their church and cause it to decay. "The very life of the church depends on her faithfulness in fulfilling the Lord's commission. To neglect this work is surely to invite spiritual feebleness and decay" (*The Desire of Ages*, p. 825).

Our churches are full of people who desire to be more spiritually dynamic. So why is it that no matter how much we saturate ourselves with praying, singing and worship, we are still spiritually wilted? How is it that so many churches are full of the walking wounded instead of a mighty army of effective witnesses? Can it be we have neglected to comprehend that spiritual growth only comes as we bear the burden of lost souls? Only through the act of leading another to understand the Word do we place ourselves in a channel to create spiritual life. "Let ministers teach church members that *in order to grow spiritually* they must carry the burden that the Lord has laid upon them—the burden of leading souls into the truth" (*Gospel Workers*, p. 200).

Before Jesus returns He will pour out His Spirit in latter rain power to take the gospel to the world. We often pray for this day to come. We study and read books on the latter rain. But what is the prerequisite for the Spirit's outpouring?

"The great outpouring of the Spirit of God, which lightens the whole earth with His glory, will not come until we have an enlightened people, that know by *experience* what it means to be *laborers* together with God. When we have entire, wholehearted consecration to the *service* of Christ, God will recognize the fact by an *outpouring of His Spirit* without measure; but this will not be while the *largest portion* of the church are not laborers together with God" (*Christian Service*, p. 253).

The Holy Spirit fills those who have an experience in laboring for God. It can't be any other way. The latter rain empowers God's people to take the gospel to the world in one last, fantastic, compelling way. It doesn't supernaturally endow us with the *ability* to witness. Instead it supercharges our witness with amplified conviction.

Occasionally people tell me their congregation is not ready to hold evangelistic meetings. They assume they need to first have a revival and correct every wrong in the church. While we do need revival and reformation, it is incorrect to think it will happen in a serviceless vacuum.

The reason churches are spiritually stagnant and immature is because the members have been staring at their own belly buttons for too long. They need to get their focus off themselves and onto the lost. As we break the bread of life to feed the spiritually starved, we stop cannibalizing our fellow church members. Soul winning solves a lot of problems.

"If they would … work to win souls to Christ, they would soon be so busy proclaiming the truth and helping the suffering that they would have no time to dissect character, no time to surmise evil and then report the results of their supposed keenness in seeing beneath the surface. ... They will forget self in the desire to save souls. They will see so much work to do, so many fellow beings to help, that they will have no time to look for faults in others. They will have no time to work on the negative side" (*Testimonies for the Church*, Vol. 8, p. 82, 83).

If revival and spiritual maturity are to be realized, we must work one-on-one with non-believers. We have to get out of our cushy Christian cocoons and learn how to share the Bible with lost people. Revival can sweep our congregations when the majority of us study the Word of God for ourselves and open its mysteries to others.

Discuss, Learn, Apply

1. What is the best medicine for the church?

2. List at least three positive things that happen in our own spiritual experience as we tell people about Jesus.

3. What is the inevitable consequence of not sharing our faith?

4. What is the prerequisite for revival and the outpouring of the Holy Spirit?

Chapter 4
THAWING FROZEN CHURCHES

One Sabbath morning I was the guest speaker in a large church. As I walked through the front door, I noticed an interesting phenomenon. Whenever I approached someone going in the opposite direction, I looked them in the eye to smile and wish them a good day, only to have them break eye contact and walk away. *"I know I'm not the most handsome person to look at, but it can't be that bad,"* I mused. *"Do I have remnants of breakfast stuck between my front teeth?"* A quick check in the bathroom mirror ruled this out, so I went to sit in the church foyer to observe how the members related to each other. What I saw comforted me that I didn't have a personal hygiene problem that no one wanted to tell me about. That aside, I found no comfort in the fact that not only did they avoid eye contact with me, they did the same with each other. Of course there were little groups of people happily visiting and having a good time. But whenever someone approached an unknown person, they instantly ducked their head. It's a wonder more people didn't bump into each other with the amount of this going on.

As a result of this experience I came up with a theory I have experimented with in numerous churches. I believe the reason many congregations feel like a Siberian winter is because the members lack social skills to speak with strangers. Another contributing factor is that many members cannot remember their fellow parishioner's names. To save themselves embarrassment because they forgot a name, they tend to avoid people.

Churches that excel at winning others have a knack to make people feel loved. Without this ability soul winning is like a quadriplegic trying to win an Olympic race. If we are to be effective witnesses we need to know how to meet, greet and make friends of people.

If you speak to the members of an ice-cold church, most of them will say they are very friendly. In fact they are—with each other. These churches are the last to realize how a lack of caring for visitors is hindering Christ's mission! Guests often go unnoticed while members gather in small clusters and merrily chat with their friends. Truly friendly churches always look for the stranger in their midst and take the initiative to strike up a conversation.

A root cause for many frozen churches is that their members are shy or hesitant to speak to strangers. You can typically warm these chilly saints

up by training them on how to converse with others. The **FORT** acronym
is a simple outline anyone can use to start conversations:

F	Family	✓ *How is your family doing?*
		✓ *Are you originally from this area?*
		✓ *In what area were you raised?*
O	Occupation	✓ *What kind of work do you do?*
		✓ *How long have you worked there?*
		✓ *What type of work did you do?*
		(retired or unemployed)
		✓ *How do you like your job?*
R	Religion	✓ *What is your religious background?*
		✓ *Have you been a* (Methodist) *all your life?*
		✓ *Do you attend a church?*
		✓ *Which church do you attend?*
		✓ *Does your whole family attend together?*
T	Testimony	✓ *My life before I accepted Christ was...*
		✓ *How I became a Christian...*
		✓ *My life since becoming a Christian...*
		✓ *I have recently been sharing with my friends some interesting Bible lessons that have meant much to me. May I share them with you?*
		(NOTE: Focus on the gospel more than on how you became an Adventist.)

Here is a sample conversation you can try the next time you see a
guest at church. (With a little adapting you can actually use this in any
social situation.) While extending your hand and smiling, say, "Hello, my
name is _____." Most people will respond with their name. If they don't,
you can say, "*What's your name?*"

"*I'm happy to meet you. I noticed you here at church today and thought
I would come over and say hello. Are you from around here?*" Wait for their
answer. If you find something you can relate to, then respond to it. For
example, if they tell you they live in the same area where you reside, you
can talk about this. A natural follow-up question would be "*How long have
you lived here?*" or "*Do you know the Smiths?*"

Once you have comfortably discussed the topic of family, you can
move to the next subject if the time and situation allow. At the end of the
conversation you can close by saying, "*It's been good visiting with you today.
I look forward to seeing you next week.*" Or you can take the relationship

a step further and introduce them to someone else. Try inviting them to join you for Sabbath lunch.

To illustrate how the most simple remedy can change a church's sociability and witnessing potential, I will tell you of a fairly large church whose members all decided to wear name tags. Every Sabbath, stick-on name tags were hung on a bulletin board near the greeters. As members arrived, they each donned their preprinted name tags with their names on them, while guests were given personalized tags handwritten by the greeters. The church later recounted to me the remarkable difference this made in their fellowship and ability to win people. Members began to instinctively look for those who had handwritten tags. Conversations among long-time members and newcomers were sparked and people were won. Of course, this approach is not necessary in a church with twelve people attending unless everyone has Alzheimer's. But if you have a hundred or more members, you may want to try it.

Another helpful tool to create a warm friendly environment, and one less obtrusive than name tags, is to display each page of your picture membership directory on a church bulletin board in the foyer. Whenever you see someone whose name you can't remember, consult this handy resource. Then you can appear to have the best of memories by greeting them by name and by having a pleasant visit with them.

The terminology you use to introduce people says a lot about how you view them and ultimately about how they will feel regarding their experience at your church. If you call them "visitors," you are telling them that you expect them to be at your church for a temporary period. However, if you call them "our special guests," they feel welcomed. An even better option is to say, "We are honored to have our new friends with us today." It is a subtle distinction that can make a huge difference in your effectiveness.

One Sabbath I was lingering in the foyer of my church after the worship service had begun. It was empty except for one greeter, who's duty it was to meet any latecomers. I was getting ready to go to the pulpit to preach when I noticed a man in blue jeans and tennis shoes come through the front door. I went over and introduced myself. He told me his name was Charles and that he was walking past our church when he decided to come in and see what our worship service was like. I asked him if he was from our area. He explained he was in the military and was in town for a couple of months for officer's training at the local Air Force base. Since he was dressed casually, he didn't feel comfortable staying for church. Smiling, I told him he looked very comfortable and that I envied him. By telling him I was the pastor and that I enjoyed seeing people dressed as he was, I was able to influence him to stay.

After the service, I warmly greeted Charles at the rear door of the sanctuary. I seized the opportunity to invite him to my house for lunch with the hope that we could get to know him. Of course, he felt a little uncomfortable accepting since this was his first time at our church. Providentially, Bill was in the line directly behind Charles and was also coming over. I introduced them to each other. Bill enthusiastically offered Charles a ride and made him feel at home. Fortunately, Charles accepted and joined us for a very enjoyable afternoon.

Over the next several weeks Bill brought Charles to church every Sabbath and took him to various members' homes for lunch. Our church showed him a lot of love while he was in town. During our time together we learned Charles was married to an Adventist even though he was not a member. A few months after Charles returned home he sent me a thrilling letter. He wrote, *"For twenty years my wife has been an Adventist and I never opened my heart to her beliefs. It took the hospitality of your church to show me what I was missing by not becoming an Adventist. When I returned home I began Bible studies and am now a baptized member. Please give my deepest thanks to all your members who made me feel at home in their church."*

I am enormously thankful I stopped to converse with Charles that Sabbath. I am more grateful for a church with people who allowed God to use them to be friendly and win someone to Christ. God has people for you and your church to meet. Take the time to learn how to talk with strangers. It will pay off in eternal rewards.

Discuss, Learn, Apply

1. How do guests feel when they attend your church?

2. How can you help guests feel more comfortable and welcome in your church?

3. What do you personally get out of this chapter? What do you want to implement? What do you want to ask God for?

4. In the next week, determine to visit a church where you don't know anyone. (To experience the full effect of what non-members feel coming to your church, try visiting a church outside of your denomination.) After your visit, write down the feelings and experiences you had. Then look at what this tells you about visitors to your church and how you can make it a more pleasant experience for them.

Chapter 5
HOW TO DOUBLE GOD'S JOY

For years I was on the front lines of personal evangelism. I preached every week, gave Bible studies, held evangelistic meetings and led people to Christ. Then I accepted a call to train others how to do what God had taught me. Every week I flew around the continent to conduct winsome witnessing seminars. It was very fulfilling until I noticed I had stopped winning people. I was spending all my time telling the saints how to be God's witness, but I had ironically ceased witnessing myself. I knew things had to change.

Because of my extremely busy travel and office schedule, I asked God to lead me to just one person who would study the Bible with me. The very next Sabbath I met a guest at my home church that accepted my offer for studies. We had a thrilling time exploring the Word together and he was baptized six months later. Not wanting to sit around for half a year twiddling my thumbs, I asked God to lead me to someone else.

Almost immediately I met an interested couple. I was walking down an aisle at the office supply store when I passed a lady going in the opposite direction. Several paces past her the thought occurred to me that she appeared familiar. I stopped and turned around to get another look. At that moment she had also turned and was staring at me. I shouted down the aisle, *"You look familiar to me. Have we ever met?" "Well, you know, I was thinking the same about you,"* she called back. We approached each other and compared notes. I learned that several years ago she had visited the church in town I used to pastor. At the time, she and her former husband were on the precipice of divorce and they hoped returning to her childhood church might mend their strained relationship. I had even once visited her at work. Unfortunately her marriage failed and she only attended church one or two times. Now several years later she was remarried.

"Although I am no longer the pastor, we have an excellent preacher that you would really enjoy. I'd love to have you come to church," I invited. Brenda looked interested. She replied, *"My husband and I have been thinking about getting back to church. We just don't know which one yet. In fact, we visited the Adventist bookstore last week and bought some books to read."* I saw this as my open door. *"Brenda, I have some studies you and your husband would enjoy. I have a hobby of giving Bible studies to people and I recently completed them with a man. I'm now looking for someone*

else. Do you think you might like to see the studies?" I inquired. Brenda thought this was a good idea and we exchanged telephone numbers. Later when I called, she invited me over to meet her husband. It wasn't long before we were studying together and they both were baptized.

At the start of every year I ask God to lead me to at least one person I can study the Bible with. Answers to my prayers are exhilarating. I find receptive people everywhere. All I need to do is ask God to surface them. "All over the world men and women are looking wistfully to heaven. Prayers and tears and inquiries go up from souls longing for light, for grace, for the Holy Spirit. *Many* are on the verge of the kingdom, waiting only to be gathered in" (*The Acts of the Apostles*, p. 109).

I can't help but believe God is happy with my small annual goal of one person. Isn't Jesus' joy in "seeing souls redeemed by His sacrifice" (*The Desire of Ages*, p. 142). Jesus says all heaven rejoices over one sinner who repents (Luke 15:7). Anticipating the joy of the redeemed in heaven helped our Saviour find strength to endure the cross (Hebrews 12:2). So every time I help even one person follow God, pleasure pulsates through the heart of heaven.

My goal as a church member is to double my membership every year by personally leading one person into the waters of baptism and church fellowship. This is not a requirement of my job and no one keeps a scorecard. I don't do it because I'm a minister. I'm extremely busy with all my activities and I don't need an extra item to squeeze into my already very crowded schedule. In fact, I can give only one hour a week to this. So why do I do it? Because I believe it makes God happy and I *know* it makes me happy.

I want to propose that you can make God twice as happy as He currently is. How? If God is ecstatic with your conversion, then think how He will feel when you lead another person to Him. By doubling your own membership every year you can double the amount of joy God receives. "*Joy* shall be in heaven over ***one sinner*** that repenteth" (Luke 15:7).

Just think of the impact we can make if every church member has this as a goal! Our congregation's memberships will double in a single year. Even if only half the church is successful, we will still experience phenomenal growth and joy.

To accomplish this, we need to think differently about evangelism. We can't focus on baptizing masses of people like a public evangelist. Instead, we must put the emphasis on winning one person at a time. If we challenge our members with achieving large numbers of conversions it will only scare most of them into becoming more firmly entrenched in their pews to wait for the professional evangelists to do the job. But if each person sets a realistic goal to influence only a single individual, then it is something everyone can see themselves doing. "It is through personal contact and association that men are reached by the saving power of the gospel. *They are not saved in masses, but as individuals.* Personal influence is a power" (*Thoughts From the Mount of Blessing*, p. 36).

This is an inspired plan. The apostle Paul used it and led the early church to experience exponential kingdom growth. "And the things that you have *heard from me* among many witnesses, commit these to *faithful men* who will be able to *teach others* also" (2 Timothy 2:2).

Notice the progression. Paul taught someone the truth. This "witness" then taught Timothy. Timothy in turn was instructed to win others and disciple them into "faithful men." Then these "faithful men" were to go and teach still others. Everyone who is won and taught shares the gospel with someone else. Under the power of the Holy Spirit, this dynamic plan resulted in explosive growth in the early church.

It can do the same today. Every member who wins one person a year and disciples them to win a soul the following year can launch their church into stratospheric doubling of their membership. "Every addition to the church should be one more agency for the carrying out of the great plan of redemption" (*Testimonies for the Church*, Vol. 8, p. 47).

Let's explore the volatile power of exponential growth. The following table compares the number of persons won by an evangelist baptizing 1,000 converts a day to that of one person winning one soul the first year, then training that person to win someone else the second year. Every year thereafter each person wins one more convert:

Gifted Evangelist wins 1,000 converts a day	Believer begins by winning one person a year
After 1 year: 365,000 converts	2 converts
After 2 years: 730,000 converts	4 converts
After 3 years: 1,095,000 converts	8 converts
After 4 years: 1,460,000	16 converts
After 5 years: 1,825,000 converts	32 converts
After 8 years: 2,920,000 converts	256 converts
23rd year: 8,395,000 converts	8,388,000 converts
24th year: 8,760,000 converts	16,777,216 converts (nearly twice that of the evangelist)

25th year: 9,125,000 converts	33,554,432 converts (nearly 3.75 times more)
26th year: 9,490,000 converts	67,108,864 converts (7 times that of the evangelist)

In just twenty-four years there are twice as many people as the evangelist. And all of this comes from simply focusing on *one* person a year. The person who has won the most converts in this illustration is the first person. They won twenty-four. But the net effect is in the millions because they've taught their converts to each win and train one person a year. Not only is there more numerical growth, but the spiritual growth of each convert is a much better quality.

Many churches have been sitting for at least a quarter of a century with the same number of people sitting in the pews week after week. One year they baptize a few people and the next year an equal number die or move. They never get ahead. This shouldn't be and doesn't have to be the story of your church.

This exponential growth of "thousands upon thousands" is exactly what inspiration says is possible when every member is witnessing to the lost. "Wherever a church is established, *all the members* should engage actively in missionary work. They should visit every family in the neighborhood and know their spiritual condition. If professed Christians had engaged in this work from the time when their names were *first* placed on the church books ... *thousands upon thousands* would today stand with God's commandment-keeping people" (*Testimonies for the Church*, Vol. 6, p. 296).

Christians in other parts of the world are already experiencing phenomenal growth. While holding evangelistic meetings in the Philippines, I saw a staggering 13,000 people baptized. This was the result of the cooperative effort of lay people giving studies, home meetings and our public seminars. Today I received a call from a friend whose mother lives in Manila where Doug Batchelor and I held this evangelistic seminar. She wanted me to know that one of the new converts from last year's meeting had just completed his first Bible seminar where eleven persons were baptized. Is it any wonder the church is growing in places like the Philippines? New members are using their gifts to propagate the gospel!

Now I think I know what someone is thinking —they are saying to themselves this massive form of response is only possible in foreign fields. Listen, before we quickly discount the relativity of what is happening overseas, we need to remember that believers in these areas are following a plan we aren't. A majority of their lay people are actively involved in witnessing. Could it be we don't win more people in developed countries because such a measly percentage of our membership is engaged in reaching the lost?

Is this all too true of us? "There are those who for a lifetime have professed to be acquainted with Christ, yet who have never made a personal effort to bring even one soul to the Saviour. They leave all the work for the minister. He may be well qualified for his calling, but he cannot do that which God has left for the members of the church" (*The Desire Ages*, p. 141).

Certainly, more people are interested in the gospel in some foreign cultures because they don't have as many of the world's distractions. But they have their own unique challenges. When preaching in third world countries, I find the people who make decisions for truth often have to choose God over earning a livelihood. In reality, this is a greater impediment to conversion than what people face in more technologically advanced societies.

The truth is if the majority of our members continue to neglect to witness, we will continue to get the same miserable results we've experienced for years. It doesn't matter which culture we are called to witness to. All hands need to be on deck in these last hours. Now is the time to commit to change. Now is the time to double God's joy.

We can have exponential conversions in North America and other industrialized countries. But it needs to begin with you and me. Will you covenant today to allow God to use you to win at least one person to Christ over the next year? This is the attainable goal I want to challenge you with. You can't do it in your own power. Yet you can cooperate with heaven by making the effort, praying for souls and learning soul-winning skills.

If this is your desire please prayerfully compete the covenant form:

My Desire

I, _____, by God's power and grace, dedicate my life to be used by Him to double my personal membership this year. I will seek to win one person to Christ and to train this person how to win a soul the following year. Understanding that there is joy in heaven over one who repents, I will participate in doubling the joy of God and angels.

Signed _____ Date _____

Discuss, Learn, Apply

1. Read again Ellen White's statement in *The Acts of the Apostles*, page 109. What does this passage mean to you personally?

2. How can you double God's joy?

3. Describe God's model for church growth found in 2 Timothy 2:2.

4. The chapter closes with the encouragement to personally commit to working for the salvation of one soul. Please read carefully the prayer at the end of this chapter. Would you like to accept this challenge? _____ List your first two steps to make this a reality.

Chapter 6
GIVE A PORTION TO SEVEN

A woman really wanted to be used by God to win someone. She attended a series of witnessing classes and prepared to give Bible studies. It wasn't long before she found a candidate in an elderly neighbor. They studied for most of a year. This lady was fervent about her mission. But despite all her hard work and sincere prayers she never had the pleasure of seeing the woman accept Christ. *"All is not lost,"* she said. *"One day my friend may yet accept the truth."* While this is a comforting thought, you could still hear the stinging disappointment in the lady's voice. She yearned to feel the joy of seeing a person converted by her effort. Because of this lack of fruit, she never ventured to give studies again. It didn't need to happen this way. What this woman forgot to factor in was two simple facts of life —the law of averages and the learning curve principle.

The learning curve principle says that when a person seeks to acquire a new skill, it will take them longer to accomplish a task than someone who has experience. A person just starting to witness is not going to be as efficient as one who has presented hundreds of studies. They are going to make mistakes, not qualify their Bible students as carefully and miss cues to get decisions. But over time a reservoir of experience will provide the skill that brings results. This is why a new Bible instructor must utilize the law of averages to help them succeed.

What the law of averages says is that if you are going to win one person, you will need to witness to and study with several. This law is at work every time we work for God and is mentioned in the Bible. "Cast thy bread upon the waters: for thou shalt find it after many days. Give a portion to seven, and also to eight; for thou knowest not what evil shall be upon the earth. ... He that observeth the wind shall not sow; and he that regardeth the clouds shall not reap. ... In the morning sow thy seed, and in the evening withhold not thine hand: for thou knowest not whether shall prosper, either this or that, or whether they both shall alike be good" (Ecclesiastes 11:1–6).

What does bread represent in Scripture? The Word of God or Jesus (John 6:35, 51, 63). And what does water signify? Masses of people (Revelation 17:15). Given these connections, consider this paraphrase of Ecclesiastes 11:1–6:

"Share the Word of God with several persons for after many days it will prosper. Give the Word to seven, and also eight. Do not limit it to only one person for you do not know what will happen. Don't wait for the ideal or perfect time to share Christ for if you do this the devil will make sure you don't find it and consequently you will not reap a harvest of souls. Wherever you go, morning or evening, share the good news of salvation, because you don't know what will prosper, either this Bible study or that one, or whether both studies will lead to a positive decision for Christ and His truth."

On every hand sow your seed for Bible studies. Don't wait for people to waltz up to you and beg you to take them to church. Do as Jesus did— seek them where they are. "He reached the hearts of people by going among them as one who desired their good. *He sought them* in the public streets, in private houses, on the boats, in the synagogue, by the shores of the lake, and at the marriage feast. He met them at their daily vocations, and manifested an interest in their secular affairs. … In order to reach all classes, we must meet them where they are. They will seldom seek us of their own accord" (*The Desire Ages*, p. 151, 152).

Remember, "*Many* are waiting to be personally addressed. In the very family, the neighborhood, the town, where we live, there is work for us to do as missionaries for Christ" (*The Desire Ages*, p. 141). Find these people. Ask God to open doors for you to offer studies to *many*. And out of the many one is sure to ripen for the harvest.

This is one of the little recognized secrets of success. Don't neglect it. If you spend the better part of a year studying with a single person and they don't make a decision you will be disappointed. However, if you are studying with several and if even one of them commits their life to God, you will find a joy and satisfaction that propels you to seek the next person to lead to Christ.

You need to examine your schedule to see how many studies you can do in a week. Plan an hour in the home of each one you give. How many hours can you dedicate in a week to search for lost people? I suggest most people dedicate three or four hours a week for the first month. Some of the people you study with during this time will drop out and it will give you the opportunity to focus on the remaining students who are the most interested and likely to follow the Lord. After the first month you should be able to get by with investing a couple hours a week.

The amount of time you need to prepare is based on the lessons you use and how much information you already know. Recognize that once you invest the time to prepare a study it is just as easy to give that same study to one person as it is to present it to five. It's like my grandmother used to say, "It is as easy to cook for ten as it is for five." In fact, the more you present the same study the more familiar you become with the material, thus making it that much simpler to present.

Full-time employed Bible instructors need to have studies in at least thirty different homes a week. When you break this down into a normal work week it simply is giving God an honest amount of work. One study takes approximately one hour to give. If you give thirty studies then you are working thirty hours a week. Full time Bible workers should plan to work at least a forty-hour week. The ten hours spent not giving studies are used to prepare and to drive to the next appointment.

Too many full-time Bible instructors get distracted with being the church's errand runner. They neglect the thing they were hired to do—give studies. They teach Sabbath School lessons, visit the sick, deliver mail and a host of other things not directly related to their job. It is no wonder when the time comes for the church to evaluate their effectiveness, they often don't discover enough conversions to warrant continuing employment.

Some people may claim 30 studies a week is an unattainable goal, yet I know from experience that it is not only doable, but it is necessary for success. This was the goal that I followed when I served as a full-time Bible instructor and it is one that I have required of my paid staff.

Doing 30 studies a week puts the law of averages to work for you. Not every study is going to materialize with someone accepting Jesus and following Him in truth. If a Bible instructor is only conducting 10 studies, they may find that at the end of their contract period the fruit is so small that the church comes to the conclusion that Bible instructors are not a good investment.

Besides distractions to their work there is another important factor commonly at work that keeps Bible instructors from conducting a large number of studies. Too often, the Bible instructor is not given the resources necessary to get many studies very quickly. Instead, they are expected to obtain studies exclusively from soliciting people door-to-door. It is no wonder that they feel 30 studies a week is impossible! One would need to knock on thousands of doors to get this many studies.

Most people are not home during the day, most people are not interested in what the stranger-at-the-door has to offer, and most Bible instructors cannot and will not keep up the pace of knocking on thousands of doors to get their 30 studies. Consequently, the Bible instructor tends to wear out and settle for a much lower number of studies—typically a dozen or less. At this point the law of averages is not on their side and they can expect around one to five baptisms as a result. Many churches determine that this is not a sufficient enough return for their investment in a Bible instructor.

I have seen this dynamic played out time after time with the same unsatisfactory results. It is rooted in the fact that the Bible instructor believes door knocking is the main method to get studies. When one is attending an evangelism training school, this may be the case—because there are too many students to get enough interest cards to cover so many Bible instructors. Once they are employed by a church, however, they must not depend on door knocking alone to meet their goal of 30 weekly studies.

I want to let you in on a powerful method to get 30 studies a week if you are a full-time Bible instructor. Gather every name of interested persons your church has available. (I describe how to do this in chapter 8.) Begin working these interests. Then, most importantly, have the church invest in mailing at least ten thousand Bible study interest cards to homes in your territory. The historical return on such cards is one to three per thousand cards mailed. Mailing ten thousand cards should give you 100 to 300 interested persons that you can visit and offer studies.

With your cards mailed back to you and a good list of names from other sources, get out and follow up all the names. (Use the Something Wonderful for You Card Canvass in the Appendix.) Be sure to put in a full day's work (eight hours a day or more of *real* work) for three to four weeks. By the end of the month you will find that you have the 30 Bible studies you need.

You may find it helpful to do what I do—I tell any hesitating prospects that I have 100 requests (or whatever the number is) and that I only have room in my schedule for 30 of them. If they want to try the studies, now is the time to schedule it, for in a week or two, I will not have room to accommodate them. This is not only a true statement, but it motivates people to make the decision to give the studies a try. I remind them that they have nothing to lose, since there is no obligation to continue the studies if it is not meeting their needs.

By mailing Bible study offer cards, you let the postman do the cold door-knocking for you. This leaves you free to visit everyone who sends back a card. Thus, your time is spent only with the people who have declared they are interested in Bible studies.

If you follow this method, you will quickly fill your schedule with 30 or more in-home studies a week and your valuable time will be spent actually *giving* studies and not out pounding the pavement trying to *get* studies. After all, the church is paying the full-time Bible instructor to give studies and not just *attempting* to get them. This is where the church needs to invest in sending the Bible study offer cards out (be sure you mail them and not just drop them off at doors for the latter method will NOT give you a good return). Some churches are so intent on saving money that they end up losing much, much more through inefficiency. Don't let your church be "penny wise" and "pound foolish." And if you are a Bible instructor, make sure you start with a large number of interests so that your time is spent wisely utilizing the law of averages to your benefit.

If you are hired as a Bible instructor, be sure you have an agreement with the church that you will focus on giving studies and will not have time for all the other things needing to be done. Set your goal of thirty studies a week and work your way up to it. If you do this, and qualify the people you study with, you will find God will give you plenty of fruit for the harvest. An effective and experienced Bible worker, giving thirty studies a week, should eventually find that fifteen to over twenty persons will be baptized and commit their lives to God. Utilizing the principle of the learning curve and the law of averages, everyone can taste the joy of a harvest.

Discuss, Learn, Apply

1. What is the learning curve principle?

2. Explain the law of averages as it relates to soul winning.

3. Please read again the statements from Ellen White in *Desire Ages*, pages 151-152 and page 141. What can we learn from Jesus?

4. Prayerfully consider how much time per week you will commit to God to give Bible studies. If you consecrate this time to God and ask him to lead you to people who are open to spiritual things, you will experience God using you. Do you believe that? If so, how much time do you want to regularly give to this work?

Chapter 7
DIVINE APPOINTMENTS

D uring my early morning devotions, I was thinking about the people who were part of a health club I had joined. I prayed, *"Lord, You know one reason I joined this club is so I can find lost souls for You. I have had a few opportunities to witness, but nothing has developed into a serious interest. Is there someone I am missing? If so, could You bring them to my attention?"*
Later that morning, I went to the gym to work out. After an hour of grueling sweat I grabbed my gym bag and began to walk out the door, looking forward to a refreshing shower at home. *"Mr. Gibbs,"* I heard someone call my name. I stopped and turned around to see the young lady who worked behind the counter. *"I wonder what she wants,"* I thought. *"Can I ask you a question?"* she asked. *"You're a minister, aren't you?"* *"Yes I am,"* I said, pondering what was coming next. *"My husband and I are looking for a church."* She continued, *"Which one do you speak at? We'd like to attend."* This sudden answer to prayer almost knocked me off my feet. I can only imagine God smiling at my utter shock at this dramatic turn of events. Perhaps He had been patiently waiting for me to ask for His help for a long time and was anxious to get started as soon as I prayed.

On another occasion I prayed, *"God, if there is someone You want me to speak to today, please make it obvious."* A few hours later I was reading a booklet on the second coming while flying home on a mostly empty 747. An inquisitive stewardess had time to make small talk and asked me what I was reading. When I told her, she surprised me with saying, *"I'm interested in Bible prophecy too."*

My automatic response was to turn the little book over and write my name and address on the back. Handing it to her, I offered, *"If you find this interesting and would like more information feel free to write me at this address."*

She graciously thanked me and returned to the back of the plane for the rest of the flight. In about sixty minutes the vibrant young woman reappeared at my side, bubbling over with excitement. Kneeling in the aisle, she enthusiastically exclaimed, *"I've read this entire book and agree with everything in it! Here is my address. Please send me anything you have."*
It was another remarkable divine appointment that God delighted to give

me. I sat in my seat completely awestruck by His love for lost souls and the power of prayer.

God's passion for saving the lost is awesome. Why else does He go to such great lengths to reach sinners? When Jesus entered Jericho He walked up to a sycamore tree and called the name of the man who had climbed it only minutes before. Even though He had never met Zaccheus, Jesus knew him by name and understood the yearning of his inner most being. This was a divine appointment arranged by the Holy Spirit (Luke 19:1-5).

God will also give you thrilling divine appointments as we seek the lost. Here is an exciting assignment. Begin praying each morning for God to bring to your attention people who are interested in spiritual things. When He answers your prayer, take it as a sign God is showing you His passion for the lost and His power to hear your petitions on their behalf. Then use the **FORT** discussion to share your testimony and enthusiastically offer Bible studies. Pray this each day until it happens. Then continue to pray for new appointments.

Discuss, Learn, Apply

1. What is God's passion?

2. What biblical examples come to your mind that shows this passion of God?

3. Plead read again the last paragraph of this chapter. What does God want to do in your life? What is your part?

4. Would you like to accept this challenge and earnestly ask God to bring you in contact with people who are looking for Him?

Chapter 8
FAVORITE FISHING HOLES
FOR SOUL WINNERS

*P*art of my childhood was spent growing up in Louisiana where there is an abundance of lakes and rivers and plenty of water sports to go along with it. With water everywhere, children learn to either fish and swim or drown. I did a little of all three as a child. As an adult, I transitioned from catching fish to watching them underwater with a scuba tank strapped to my back and an air hose stuck in my mouth.

One day, I was scuba diving off a rock jetty in the turquoise waters of Panama City, Florida, near where I used to live. This spot was also a favorite place for fisherman. The top of it was lined with sunburned anglers with their poles in hand and lines dangling in the water. What they didn't realize was that sixty feet below the surface I was making my way past their lures. As I slowly swam along admiring the beauty that proliferates in the underwater world, a bright silvery object reflecting the sunlight caught my attention. I finned my way over and discovered a tiny half-dead bait fish with a hook in it and an almost invisible fishing line snaking towards the surface.

It struck me as humorous that there wasn't a fish within fifty feet of this fisherman's line. In fact, the current was so swift that all the fish had found a nice protective cove of rocks to shelter in and were not coming out anytime soon. I imagined the fishermen on the jetty who had been waiting for hours in the blazing sun for a solitary bite on their line. From my cool underwater perspective, I knew they were in for a long and boring day if I didn't pump a little excitement into their lives. I carefully reached out so I wouldn't get hooked and grabbed the line with my gloved hand and gave it several strong pulls. Later, as I walked along the top of the rocks, I overheard the fishermen talking about the one bite of the day that came from a monster-sized fish that got away. I am sure the size of that elusive fish only grew as the story was repeated at home that evening.

Frequent fishermen have their favorite fishing holes. They catch more in these familiar spots because they understand the fish's behavior—what they like to eat, when they bite and where they like to rest and nest. Winning souls is a lot like fishing. There are favorite places where you can always find a good catch of people for the Lord.

Just as all fish aren't alike and require different lures to entice them, not one method will work for everyone, because people are different. In this chapter I will share with you several approaches that are being successfully used to lead people into the kingdom of God.

One of the most inexpensive ways to obtain a study is to visit people who respond to one of our Christian television or radio programs or other Christian media. Ministries like *Hope Channel, Amazing Facts, It Is Written, Voice of Prophecy* and many others spend millions each year to proclaim the three angels' message over the airwaves and in print. Thousands graduate from their Bible correspondence courses and receive the free literature offered on their programs. Many of these individuals are excellent contacts for the kingdom.

Don't repeat the oversight some make concerning media responses. One pastor told me he didn't find these names to be of any value. *"None of them are ready to be baptized and few even remember the program,"* he complained. He missed the point. The names you receive from media ministries are contacts to be nurtured into a Bible study. It is a happy bonus when you do find a person who is ready for baptism just from the media alone.

The *Media Survey* in the appendix helps me determine if a person is a good candidate for Bible studies. It is simple to use and self-explanatory. All you need to do is visit the media interest and introduce yourself as outlined on the survey. Be sure to smile, smile, smile. Explain that you are taking a brief survey of three questions for the television (or radio) program and that their help is greatly appreciated. If you find an opportunity to enter the home and do the survey you will be more effective. At the end of your questions you will offer them free Bible studies. A more detailed explanation of how to offer the studies is described on the survey.

Here is something to consider as you go fishing for souls. This applies to any method you use. Not everyone will respond to your offer. In fact, you don't want everyone to respond. You are seeking only those the Holy Spirit has prepared. You may get several negative answers before you find this person. This is OK. Don't let it trouble you. Picture yourself as a miner searching for a rich vein of gold. Miners blast through a lot of rock before they find gold. If you keep digging and contacting people, you eventually will hit pay dirt.

There is another very fruitful field that is often overlooked. Visitors to our churches usually go uncontacted. Every church should have a winsome system for contacting every visitor and offering them studies. I have many positive responses when doing this. During Sabbath School one week, I saw a man I did not recognize. I introduced myself and discovered his name was Joe. I learned Joe's sister was a good friend of mine and that I had baptized her. Early the next week, I phoned Joe to invite him to lunch so that we could get better acquainted. During our conversation he shared with me the pain he was feeling over his recent divorce and that he was seeking a church that followed God's truth. This opened the door for me to offer Joe my studies. We began studying together and six months later he was baptized.

This is an appropriate ministry for the church greeters to run. Instead of viewing themselves as bulletin dispensers, greeters can be God's ambassadors to find guests who can be reached with the gospel. The *Church Visitors Canvass* in the appendix has a description of how to contact church guests. Every church should be doing a ministry like this.

Former and inactive members are a special field of labor that can be very rewarding. To be involved in this ministry requires us to listen non-judgmentally and not be defensive of the church.

I was out visiting a member who had not been in church for over ten years. I opened the creaky fence gate. It sounded as though it hadn't been lubricated in quite a long time. I casually walked to the front door and knocked. When Joyce, my inactive member, opened the door, she looked very puzzled. *"How did you get to the door without my dogs tearing you to pieces?"* she asked. Alarmed, I nearly knocked her over in my rush to dive inside the house for protection. I told her the angels must be protecting me and pleaded with her to quickly let me in before the angels "changed shifts."

As we sat in Joyce's living room I explained the purpose of my visit. *"Joyce, there are many Adventists who no longer go to our church. Some leaders estimate forty to fifty percent of our membership doesn't regularly attend. There is a reason for this and I am hoping to learn from our members who don't make it to church. I suspect there are things we can do better to minister to people. Would you do me a favor by answering the questions on this simple survey I have? I really value your input and it would be a great help as we seek to do a better job at being God's church in this community."*

Joyce showed some hesitation at first. She told me her experience at our church had been so extremely painful that whenever she drove past our building she had to look in the other direction so as not to reopen the wound in her heart. I expressed the fact that I was sorry to hear this and how I wished we could become a source of hope for hurting people. Joyce consented to do the survey and showed some willingness to reconnect with the church. After a long period of healing she began to attend again. She developed new friendships and became an active part of our fellowship. (A copy of the *Former and Inactive Members Survey* is in the appendix.)

When visiting with inactive and former members, you must remember not to judge them. If I had tried to defend the church's actions that caused Joyce so much pain, she would not have listened to me. It is best to simply apologize with no excuses attached.

Sometimes inactive members will test your willingness to accept them as they are. I was visiting with a former head deacon who had not been in church for many years. During his time out he studied most of the world's religions and concluded that they all possessed some redeeming values. *"Pastor,"* he asked, *"don't you think that all of these religions are after the same thing? Don't you think God is going to save us all?"* I knew the reason Phil left the church was because of ministry burnout and he had been caught in the turbulence of a denominational-wide shaking several years ago. I didn't want to disagree with him during my very first visit. *"That's a good question, Phil. The Bible tells us that there will be people in heaven who have never heard of the gospel story but who will be saved. Here in Zechariah 13:6 we read, 'And one shall say unto him, What are these wounds in thine hands? Then he shall answer, Those with which I was wounded in the house of my friends.' I am sure there are honest people in all religions that God will ultimately lead to Himself."*

Of course, there is much more to this topic than what I covered at that point but this was enough for the moment. Phil was satisfied and began Bible studies with me. We had a wonderful time studying together and he later joyfully returned to the church to become an elder. This illustrates again the importance of not judging people or trying to correct all of their errors on the spot. When Phil told me he was comforted with the thought that his recently deceased mother was in heaven, I didn't tell him his theology was wrong. Instead I sympathized with him. Later, when we studied on where a man goes when he dies, Phil confessed, *"Pastor, when a person is out of the church for a long time, it is amazing how much of what they know to be true is forgotten."*

Some people reading this are saying, *"Now wait a minute! We need to cry aloud and spare not!"* They are determined to set everyone straight no matter how many people they run over to do it. If you are such a person, you need to consider Jesus' example. There were many things He chose to leave unsaid because He knew people couldn't bear it. Even when His brothers urged Him to go up to the feast He said, "Go ye up unto this feast:

I go not up yet unto this feast; for my time is not yet full come" (John 7:8). Jesus didn't explain to his misguided and unconverted family that He really did intend to go to the feast, but He wasn't going to go in the open manner they suggested. He just let things be. "But when his brethren were gone up, then went he also up unto the feast, not openly, but as it were in secret" (John 7:10). There is a time and season to correct your student's poor doctrine. I wish every church would develop members who know how to sensitively work with these hurting people.

A more expensive, but certainly, very useful way to get studies is to mail a card offering free Bible study guides. My favorite through the years has been the *Something Wonderful For You Card*. It is very generic in what it offers. This is what makes it so effective. I like to mail 5,000 to 10,000 of these cards to people in my city. Depending on the nature of your area, you can expect to have at least one to ten cards returned per thousand you mailed. You will significantly increase your responses to this card if you mail them to people from our media programs, guests who have attended church or anyone else on your church's mailing list. (As I mentioned previously, names can be obtained from the various church media ministries). Write a cover letter explaining the Bible study offer and include the card for them to return to you if they would like to take advantage of this free offer. For maximum results, pay the media ministries to mail the cards to their names using their letterhead.

While this method takes a fair amount of people skills, it is extremely worthwhile. I use this approach every time I desire a lot of Bible studies before an evangelistic meeting. When I first started using the Bible cards, I was a bundle of twisted nerves as I went to the doors. But after I developed what to say, how to say it and what to leave unsaid, I found a large number of the cards turned into quality studies. I've had the joy of seeing hundreds of people baptized from this source and I highly recommend it. The *Something Wonderful For You Card Canvass* in the appendix contains a complete script that I developed after visiting hundreds of homes. It works extremely well and has helped many people to find Bible studies.

A less expensive way to reach people is by going door-to-door and asking them to help you with a short survey. Now I know door-to-door solicitation is about as high on your list of favorite things to do on a day off as getting a root canal. I must confess that I don't care for it either. It invites too much rejection. But I mention it because so many people find it successful. If you remember you are hunting for the one diamond, the one person who is seeking for truth, you can find the stamina to endure many closed doors. The *Community Religious Survey* in the appendix is excellent for this purpose. Contacts from this method generally are best worked as drop-off studies at first. You can try to turn them into sit-down studies later after they've had time to know you. (Chapter 14 explains how to do drop-off and sit-down studies.)

The children in our church and schools should not be neglected. Most parents and educators welcome someone to study with their children. Too many young adults feel cheated that they were baptized without first receiving a full-message study. They often confess that they were baptized only because their friends were also doing it.

Let's not fool ourselves. Children can understand this message. I have taught them the simpler prophecies of Daniel and Revelation and the significance of being God's boy or girl in these last days. An emphasis on how to have a life-long relationship with God and how to make successful choices will help them understand the proper role of the Bible's lifestyle standards.

Two other useful approaches found in the appendix include the *Circle of Influence Canvass* and the *Letter to Family and Friends*. Both utilize the method Jesus used with the women at the well. He asked this woman a favor and thereby opened her heart to receive His teaching (John 4:7–15).

Tell others that you are taking a course to help you learn your Bible better and that one of your assignments is to find someone who will take these lessons with you. Then ask the person if they will do you a favor and assist you with this assignment. Many of your family and friends have been waiting for a way to learn more about our beliefs without feeling like you are trying to convert them. This helps to dissolve that barrier and enables them to feel good about doing you a favor. This is superb for reaching your loved ones.

No matter which methods you use, you will want to possess a positive and relaxed atmosphere. Be genuinely friendly. These are not gimmicks to be parroted in a robotic manner. With a smile brightening my face, I tell people I enjoy giving studies and that it is a hobby of mine. I explain that studying the Bible with others helps me to grow in my Christian faith and that people tell me they benefit from the studies. If it is obvious that you enjoy what you are doing, others will relax and engage with you.

Your assignment is to use one or two of these favorite fishing holes for soul winners over the next few weeks. Cast your line into people's lives and watch what the Lord allows you to bring to Him.

Discuss, Learn, Apply

1. Why do we need different methods to reach people?

2. Please write down two or three ways to find Bible studies. Explain under which circumstances you can use them to find spiritually interested people and why you think they will work in this context.

3. How do you deal with the fact that not everyone will accept your offer to study the Bible?

4. Read again the next to last paragraph of this chapter. How would you explain to someone why you want to study the Bible with them and why they should accept this offer?

Chapter 9
JESUS' METHOD WORKS!

several years ago my wife, Sherilyn, and I moved to a new neighborhood. In our new house we knelt and asked God to permit us to win our neighbors to Him. I had recently realized that if I was going to lead my members to be winsome witnesses, I needed to reach people in circumstances similar to what they faced. I was an experienced evangelist, Bible instructor and pastor, but I had never won co-workers or neighbors. This was mostly due to the fact that my co-workers were all Christians and I didn't take time for my neighbors because I spent it all with the church. This move was to begin a drastic change in approach for me.

When my neighbor, Jack, introduced himself to me, he added, *"Don't worry about mowing your lawn. I used to mow it for the former owner and I don't mind mowing for you."* While this was a generous offer, I did own a new lawn mower and enjoyed the exercise. Jack insisted in spite of my polite protests. I could use the extra time, I reasoned, so I didn't press my case any further. (Not to mention it's pretty dumb to turn down an offer from someone who will mow your lawn for free!) I kindly accepted his offer without even thinking about what was on the horizon.

It was early Sabbath morning when Sherilyn and I were lying in bed and we heard the lawn mower buzzing outside our window. My dear wife asked me what the noise was. *"I think it is Jack mowing our lawn,"* I dolefully replied. She didn't need to point out to me that it was Sabbath and our house sat on a highway that several members used to go to church. What would they think if they saw their new pastor's lawn being mowed on Sabbath? Of course, this was the least of my concerns, but it was amusing to consider.

I unsuccessfully tried to convince Sherilyn to go outside and tell Jack about the Sabbath. Not wanting to offend him, I opted instead to pray that God would somehow get the message through to him. (If He chose for me to be the messenger I would do it, but I first was going to give God the opportunity.)

I never had to talk to Jack about it because he never mowed my lawn again on Sabbath. Months later Jack profusely apologized for that first Sabbath. He explained how he later observed how I kept the Sabbath holy and how badly he felt about the incident. Because of the intense conviction God gave him, Jack not only changed his mowing schedule for me but he changed it for everyone on his list. Prayer is always the first and best option for handling difficult situations.

Over time, our two families developed a close friendship. Whenever we had a need Jack was right there to help us. We tried to reciprocate. One day we drove up to our house to find Betty, Jack's wife, sobbing at our front door. Their little dog of thirteen years had just died and Betty had come to us to find comfort. Between sobs, she choked out, *"I know little Tinker* (their toy poodle) *is in doggie heaven, but it hurts so much to lose him."* For a very brief moment I considered giving Betty a study on the state of a dog in death. But then my better judgment prevailed and told me this was an opportunity to sympathize and not sermonize. So, I wisely settled for words of consolation. *"Betty, I know the Lord is very sorry you've lost Tinker. He never wanted there to be death. Can I pray with you that God will comfort you?"*

Through this experience I realized that we had reached the place where Jack and Betty had confidence in us. Why else would they come and share such a personal grief? This was my cue to invite them to church and to take Bible studies. They readily accepted the invitation and we were blessed to baptize both of them.

This type of winsome witnessing is based on Jesus' method of soul winning. Rescuing people from sin doesn't consist only in telling people the truth. If it did, God would have erected a cosmic neon-lighted billboard in the sky to declare the truth in a take-it or leave-it fashion. Instead, Jesus joined the human family and rooted redemption in relationships. He had to become one with us if He was to win our confidence and show us the path back to God.

Jesus' life is an example of how He wants to use us to rescue lost people. We are instructed "to learn from Christ the science of soul saving" (*Review and Herald*, March 30, 1905). His method is described in one of my favorite books. "Christ's method alone will give true success in reaching the people. The Savior mingled with men as one who desired their good. He showed His sympathy for them, ministered to their needs, and won their confidence. Then He bade them, 'Follow Me'" (*The Ministry of Healing*, p. 143).

Notice there are three simple steps to Jesus' saving strategy. He first mingled with lost people as one who cared for them and desired their good. Socializing is where we also are to start. This is not partying for pleasure, but is socializing with a holy purpose. Some Christians treat lost people like hazardous waste and isolate themselves. At the other extreme are those who venture so close to the lost that they become like them in character and aren't different enough to pull them to safety. Both extremes are ineffective witnesses. Jesus' method is to get close enough to save. "While we should cultivate sociability, let it not be merely for amusement, but for a purpose. There are souls to save" (*Testimonies for the Church*, Vol. 5, p. 599).

Jesus' second step was to sympathize with others. As He socialized and discovered the hurts and needs of people, He expressed His heartfelt sympathy. He allowed people to see that he genuinely cared for them and understood their deepest longing.

His sympathy naturally led to the third step. He served people in practical ways by ministering to their needs. He fed the hungry, healed the sick and encouraged the despondent. Jesus was constantly looking for ways to serve and relieve suffering.

These three steps of socializing, sympathizing and serving naturally caused people to have confidence in Him. Once He won their confidence, Jesus invited them to follow Him in salvation.

Don't overlook this vital point. Jesus only invited people to follow Him after He first won their confidence. Effective soul winners all do the same. A person will open their heart to listen to what you have to say once they trust you and feel you have no other motive than to help them.

If we neglect to win confidence, people will be defensive when we witness to them. I have seen this repeated many times. A Christian will work alongside a co-worker for years and never make an effort to befriend them. Then when an evangelist comes to town, he will take his co-worker an advertising handbill and invite him to the meetings. In most instances the co-worker never attends. It is far more effective to start with socializing, sympathizing and serving our co-worker. People will gladly accept our invitations once they believe we want what is best for them and are not out to get something in return. This is what confidence building and Jesus' method are all about. Jesus "gains access to the heart by securing sympathy and confidence, making all feel that His identification with their nature and interest is complete" (*Evangelism*, p. 140).

Establishing confidence can be done in a variety of ways. I had made an appointment with Al for Bible studies. When I arrived for the first study, Al told me he had a question to pose before we began. *"Why are you studying with me? What do you want out of this?"* Al was testing me. Could I be trusted or was I trying to serve my own selfish purpose by getting him to join my church? He wanted to know if I had an ulterior motive. I responded, *"Al, this is a great question and I'm glad you asked it.*

I like to study with people for two reasons. First, I find it's a blessing to me. I grow spiritually from sharing God's Word. Second, I find others like what we study. So we both are blessed. If I can help you learn your Bible better and come closer to God, then I will feel it has been time well spent." Al smiled, *"That's a great answer! Let's start then."* I had passed the confidence test.

If our motive for studying with others is to fill our pews or to prop up a dying church, then we don't have the heart of Christ. We are God's witnesses because we love people and don't want them to be lost. On the positive side, we want them to enjoy the vibrant relationship with Christ that we experience. When our motives are transparent, people will intuitively trust us.

I often pray for others using the "Christ's method alone" statement. I ask the Lord to show me how I can best mingle with the person I seek to win. Then I pray God will give me opportunities to sympathize and serve them. Through it all I ask for help to win their confidence so I can offer them the bread of life.

In today's world, most people are extremely wary of religious people who aren't *closet* Christians. They are afraid they will be tricked into joining a cult. In order to qualify you as a "safe" person, one of the first questions they will ask is, *"Which church are you with?"* What they really want to know is, *"Are you safe to study with?" "Are you a member of a fringe religious group or cult?"*

There are many situations where I will answer this question by telling people my denomination. I will immediately follow this with, *"Have you heard of my church and do you know what we believe?"* After their answer, I will say, *"We often get confused with some non-Christian groups, but we are really much like any other Christian church. May I share with you a quick summary of our four main beliefs?"* If they give me permission, I will share with them our Four Cs. (See sidebar.) This establishes me as a Bible-believing Christian.

In a few select situations, I avoid being too specific about denomination. This is especially true if I am going door-to-door, visiting media responses or Bible study request cards.

We are not to be ashamed of our denominational affiliation. Not everyone, however, knows what Seventh-day Adventists believe. Sometimes we are confused with unwelcome cultic groups like the Mormons and Jehovah Witnesses.

Even if they don't have a prejudice against your church, as soon as we mention denominationalism, people think, *"The only reason they are saying these things is that they want me to join their church."* This causes

---

FOUR Cs

CHRIST. Jesus is the divine Son of God. God made in the form of man. He is the Eternal Self-Existent One and is NOT a created being. He is fully God. Jesus is the one who created the world in six days and rested the seventh day (Hebrews 1:1–3; Colossians 1:16–18).

CROSS. God the Father, in His Son, paid the penalty for man's sin on the Cross of Calvary (2 Corinthians 5:19). Only Jesus, the Sinless One, could pay our sin-debt. "The wages of sin is death" (Romans 6:23). By believing on Him and accepting the grace of His shed blood we receive the gift of eternal life. "Not of works, lest any man should boast" (Ephesians 2:9).

COMMANDMENTS. Because we love Jesus for His sacrificial death, we want to obey Him as He commands in John 14:15. We are not saved by our works. But, because we are saved, we choose to keep His commandments as the guide for successful living. (This next part is to be shared only if the person inquires about the Sabbath: *"This is the reason we go to church on Saturday, the Bible Sabbath"* (Exodus 20:8–11). *"The Sabbath was changed from Saturday to Sunday long after the New Testament record."*)

COMING AGAIN. We are a people who understand Bible prophecy. Prophecy reveals that Jesus is coming again very soon.

---

them to put up mental roadblocks and keeps them from learning the Bible with an open mind. Prejudice against organized religions has spawned a huge amount of supposedly "non-denominational" churches and made them very popular. People have a natural bias against denominations so if I need to avoid it, I do.

This next point can be easily misunderstood, so please listen patiently. If we try to get studies with the intention of adding members to our church, they will feel that we are serving our own selfish purpose. We will not be able to win their confidence as Jesus did. However, if we have the goal of helping them understand their Bible better and to grow closer to Jesus, then people will trust us. Which church they attend will be a decision they will make in relationship with the Spirit.

Someone may ask, *"Don't you want them to join God's remnant church?"* The answer is obvious—yes! But it is my hope that joining is the by-product of their having learned the Bible and grown closer to Jesus. If they join without this then I have not helped them or the church.

God will lead His children to His church if He wants them there. Our role is to share the everlasting gospel of the three angels' message (Revelation 14:6–12). The Holy Spirit will then convict them of the truth. Yes, we will explain the truth and encourage them to obey God. But ultimately each person will make their own decision and we will respect their decision even if we don't agree with it.

By avoiding denominational labels, we are not trying to be deceptive. Our church has nothing to hide. The reality is we don't want people to focus on this because of the natural prejudice that exists against all organized religions. We want them to study the Bible for what it says. We are not trying to make people Seventh-day Adventists. Our goal is to help them become followers of Jesus Christ. With a conscience enlightened by the Bible, God will convict and lead them to where they should worship. Do I believe He'll guide them to His remnant church? You bet I do. But to get into denominational labels before this happens can result in closing the door to the Spirit.

Here is what I say to people that I am visiting to get studies: *"Mary, you need to know who you are studying with. There are many groups today that don't believe in the Bible and Jesus like most of us Christians. Let me assure you I am a Bible-believing Christian who trusts that Jesus Christ is God and the Son of God. He came to this world and lived a perfect life and then died on the cross to pay the penalty for our sins. Of course, I attend a church I am very proud of, and I don't mind sharing with you where I like to attend. But this isn't the purpose of our study together. I'd rather stay away from denominationalism for now. The thing I like to focus on is teaching what the Bible says. I believe God has people in every church. My goal is to help people learn how to study the Bible for themselves. When I can show someone the tools to unravel the Bible's meaning then I feel like I've been successful. I want to ultimately become useless to my students. So when you are studying the Bible alone someday and you can't understand what you are reading, you will remember something you learned from our studies that will help you find the meaning. I feel that the most important thing for all Christians is to know their Bibles better, don't you? Is this okay with you?"*

When I introduce my denomination like this, *before* they have a chance to ask me which church I am with, they visibly relax. In most cases they are more than willing to take studies and they are more receptive to the Bible's teachings. This philosophy and mindset will enable you to get beyond people's natural defenses and wariness about cults.

This approach is not for you if you see it as a cheap gimmick. You must truly believe what you tell them. In your heart you must sincerely feel that your mission is to help them know their God and Bibles better. The Holy Spirit will lead them to His Church. When they come under conviction, then you will be there as a friend to encourage them to trust and obey Jesus.

Do you want to hear an amazing fact? Satan is happy for people to join the church. That's right. You read it correctly. It is sobering to realize, but even the devil is trying to get some people to join. If he can bring an unconverted person in, he can use them as his most effective agents to divert others. "But great care should be exercised in accepting members into the church; for Satan has his specious devices through which he purposes to crowd false brethren into the church, through whom he can work more successfully to weaken the cause of God" (*Review and Herald*, January 10, 1893).

I want to cooperate with the Spirit of God when it comes to leading a person to join the remnant. This is why I can put this topic off until I later see how they respond to truths such as salvation, the Sabbath, the judgment, mark of the beast and the call out of Babylon. If they manifest conviction, then I will work where God is working in their life. Until then, the denominational issue is a back-burner issue.

"In laboring in a new field, do not think it your duty to say at once to the people, We are Seventh-day Adventists; we believe that the seventh day is the Sabbath; we believe in the non-immortality of the soul. This would often erect a formidable barrier between you and those you wish to reach. Speak to them, as you have opportunity, upon points of doctrine on which you can agree. Dwell on the necessity of practical godliness. Give them evidence that you are a Christian, desiring peace, and that you love their souls. Let them see that you are conscientious. Thus you will gain their confidence; and there will be time enough for doctrines. Let the heart be won, the soil prepared, and then sow the seed, presenting in love the truth as it is in Jesus."

(*Gospel Workers*, p. 119, 120).

Discuss, Learn, Apply

1. Please name and briefly explain the three steps of Jesus' method. What did Jesus do after these three steps?

2. How can you apply these three steps in your association with people?

3. Please list the four pillars of our faith and describe in your own words how you would explain them to someone not of your faith.

4. "We do not do missionary work in order to win members for our church." What do you think about this statement? Explain your answer.

Chapter 10
ORGANIZING FOR SUCCESS

*T*he pastor gave me a large beat-up shoebox overflowing with cards and letters from non-members requesting information about our beliefs. As I sifted through the tattered papers, I discovered that most of them dated back five to seven years and had come from people who had responded to our television and radio programs. This shoebox was a mixed blessing. It was great to have the names of so many interested persons but it was also quite heartbreaking since none of them had been visited. I looked at the mountain of lost opportunities and pondered how things might be different for many of these people if we had reached them years ago.

Fortunately, one lady, whose card was in that box, was patient enough to wait for us. I could hardly believe it. When I arrived at her home, she welcomed me like a long-lost friend. Five years earlier she had taken studies with one of our media ministries and believed everything we taught. The Jehovah's Witnesses had been to her house many times and she repeatedly refused their requests for studies because she had faith that we would one day get to her. I was relieved that she had waited. She was a delightful woman and readily accepted the entire message and was baptized.

When I first received the shoebox there were over two hundred names in it. To complicate matters, we had mailed several thousand cards to the community offering free Bible study guides. How was I going to follow up on the multitude of requests?

What I did next has helped me many times to systematically focus on getting to the most interested persons. If you are dealing with a large quantity of names, or if you are working with multiple Bible study teams, you will find this detailed, yet simple system of organizing the cards helpful. This is especially useful for a church or person who is going to give a large number of Bible studies. If you are studying with just one or two persons that you've already identified, most of this information is not relevant and you may want to only skim it.

Gathering Names

Media ministries will happily provide you with the names of their interests for you to contact. *Amazing Facts, It Is Written* and *The Voice of*

Prophecy are fruitful places to obtain names. (While I will outline the best way to get this information, it isn't always applicable to every ministry since management and methods sometimes change.)

When you contact a ministry you should ask if they will send you the list of their interests on peel and stick labels. This is far more preferable to a printout since you can put the peel and stick labels on index cards that can be easily organized in an index card file box. This will keep you from having to retype all the names. There may be a nominal charge for this service.

You will also want to request that the ministry give you only names active in the past eighteen months. People move so frequently today that you can waste a lot of time chasing down old addresses.

When you call the ministry, have your target zip codes ready. Most ministries will only give you the names of people who have graduated from their Bible school and inactive Bible students. They will often also provide you with the names of people who have requested the free offers from their programs. The media response names can be separate from the Bible school names. So be sure to speak to both departments. Your best potential students will be the graduates of the correspondence courses.

Another excellent alternative is to ask the media ministry to mail your Bible study offer card along with a cover letter on their stationary to all their contacts in your area. You can pay them for the cost to do this. The enclosed Bible cards can be addressed to return to you. This will save you all the time associated with other methods and it will give you a fresh list of only the names of truly interested persons. The media ministry may prefer this as well, since it safeguards their list and protects them from interests' complaints over giving their names out for solicitation.

Ordering Studies

The next thing to do is to stock a supply of study guides. You may want to get a few different types to meet the variety of needs you will find among the people you meet.

Order more of the first three or four lessons. You will use several times as many of these early lessons than of the latter ones because people will drop out over time. If you anticipate having one hundred names of interested persons, order the following: 125 of lessons one through three; 75 of lessons four through seven; 50 of lessons eight through the end. (For which lessons to use, see the chapter *Which Studies Should I Use?*)

Order other materials such as the many small doctrinal books by *Amazing Facts*. They are excellent for your own study and for giving to a student who has more questions than you have time or knowledge to answer. Mark Finley's handbook *Studying Together* is an invaluable resource everyone should have at their fingertips. Both are available from Adventist Book Centers and other bookstores.

I also like to have several copies of the *Have You Heard of the Four Spiritual Laws?* booklet on hand. (Published by Campus Crusade for Christ. Available for purchase and online in multiple languages at www. CampusCrusade.com.) This little tract presents the plan of salvation in an easy-to-understand format. It enables you to easily lead a person to Christ. You can order these from most any Christian bookstore.

Ministering Two by Two

"And He called the twelve to Himself, and began to send them out two by two, and gave them power over unclean spirits"

(Mark 6:7. NKJV).

"Two are better than one ... for if they fall, one will lift up his companion ... though one may be overpowered by another, two can withstand him, and a threefold cord is not quickly broken"

(Ecclesiastes 4:9–12. NKJV).

"Jesus bade them go out two and two through the towns and villages. None were sent forth alone, but brother was associated with brother, friend with friend. Thus they could help and encourage each other, counseling and praying together, each one's strength supplementing the other's weakness. ... It was the Saviour's purpose that the messengers of the gospel should be associated in this way. In our own time evangelistic work would be far more successful if this example were more closely followed"

(*The Desire of Ages*, p. 350).

Organizing Your Team

It is always best to have a partner to work with you. This is the method Jesus used when He sent out the disciples and it is still helpful in today's context.

Husband and wife teams are ideal since the family can minister together and bond with the students. A parent partnering with their preteen or teenage child is a good option. This exposes a child to a ministry that will shape their life. You can also partner with someone else in the church that shares your interest.

There are a few agreements you should have with your partner. Agree ahead of time on who will give the study in the home. It doesn't have to be the same person in each home. You may be the key person in one home and your partner in the next. Once you choose who is going to lead out in a study, it is best to stay with it unless there is a reason to change. Try to remain consistent since you are building relationships.

If you present the study, your partner is the silent praying partner. In most instances they should not interject their comments unless directly asked by you or the student. If both you and your partner continuously offer explanations your student may feel outnumbered. It will also be difficult to keep the study on track. This can seem like a simple matter, but it is an important one that affects the outcome.

You and your partner should frequently pray together for your students. You will always want to pray before you go out on a study. Afterwards, it is good to ask the silent partner for their thoughts and observations. This will help you get objective feedback.

It should go without saying, but you and your partner should never argue, disagree or contradict one another in the presence of your students. In case of unforeseen circumstances, work by yourself rather than disappoint your student by not arriving for an appointment. If you are not able to make it, have your partner give the study in your absence. This will inspire your student to always be present.

In the majority of cases it is not recommended to have more than you and your partner present in a student's home. It also is not wise to frequently change partners. You want to develop a rapport with your student and consistency is important to achieving this goal.

Dress When Giving Studies

While your local culture may impact what you wear on a Bible study, there are some general guidelines you should consider. These are especially helpful during your initial visit to establish studies. First impressions are lasting and influence the response we get from others. Therefore, you want to dress in a way that best represents Christ and doesn't distract from the holy and important work you are doing.

Dress should neither look like you just came from church, nor that you came from a picnic in the park. Clean dress shoes (no tennis shoes or sandals), casual pressed slacks (avoid jeans) and a nice button up shirt are appropriate for men. This is sometimes described as "smart casual."

Women's dress, whether it is slacks or a dress, should also follow this guide. Too formal a dress will frighten people and too casual will hinder your gaining respect and confidence. In our very informal culture I have seen young men dressed in short pants, tee shirts and sandals with no socks visit complete strangers and invite them to take studies. This is not recommended and it typically results in losing studies.

How to Make Student Cards

The following method assumes you do not have a computer. If you can do this electronically, you will find it very helpful. Otherwise, follow these instructions to make it easier to follow up the cards you accumulate. Get a dependable volunteer to put the students' address information on index cards. Each card needs:

✓ **Name, street address, and mailing address.** (Use peel and stick labels from media sources if available.)

✓ **Source of interest.** (i.e. Amazing Facts, It Is Written, Voice of Prophecy, Faith for Today, etc.)

✓ **Any Bible study courses the person has taken or is currently taking.** Include the date the person graduated from the course.

✓ **Date of students' last contact** with ministry providing the name.

✓ **Any other pertinent information.** (Time they're home, friends or relatives in the church, etc.)

If you work with Bible study offer cards (i.e. *Something Wonderful For You Card*), you do not need to transfer the names to index cards. Use the returned card as your working address card.

If you have a large number of cards, you will want to get a good map. Find one large enough for you to read the street names easily. If you are in a metropolitan area, a book map may be your best option.

Plot on the map the addresses on the cards as follows:

✓ **Sort the cards by zip codes.** Then give each card an individual code number. Write this number in the upper right corner of the card. The first card is given a number 1, the second card is numbered 2, the third is 3, etc.

✓ **Next, look up the street address of each card in the map index** and write the map grid-number under the code number you've written on the face of the card. Each card should end up with a code number and map grid number where the street is located. Write this in small print if you are using the *Something Wonderful For You Cards*. You will be showing these cards to your student when you visit them the first time and you don't want your notes raising suspicions of your being a stalker.

✓ **Once you have each card properly referenced, turn to the map and find the street addresses.** Use a highlighter to mark the street name on the map and write the code number that corresponds to that card by the highlighted street name. Some maps indicate the street block numbers. If your map has this, write the card's code number in the street-block corresponding with the street address. (For example if the street address is 2234 Maple Drive, you will put the card-code number on the map in the 2200 block of Maple Dr.) Draw a circle around the number on the map.

✓ **Follow this procedure with all cards.** When you finish, you will be able to see where all your potential students live by the numbers written on the map. Now you can organize the visitation into areas by pulling the cards whose numbers are in the same location.

✓ **If you're working with several teams, make photocopies of the map to give to them for their visits.** Choose ten cards in the same geographic area. Photocopy the area of the map that has these ten cards plotted upon it. Attach the cards and give it to the team members. They now can go out and visit these homes without having to crisscross the city, since all of their names have been geographically localized.

✓ **If you are working with several teams, you may want to keep a master list of all the names and addresses** along with which teams are responsible for them.

Keep a record of your visits on the back of the student's card. I typically write the date and time of my visit, if I found them home and what study I gave. This is helpful if I am studying with numerous persons and it is a good record for others to have if for some reason someone else ever needs to visit the student.

If you have numerous cards to visit a simple index card box is a good way to keep organized. I like to have several tab dividers in my index box. The topic headings are as follows:

✓ **One divider for each day of the week.** Once you have an appointment for a study, place the card behind the proper day's divider.

✓ **Telephone Calls.** This is for cards you need to follow up with a phone call.

✓ **Not Interested.** For those who have told you they are not interested.

✓ **Active Cards.** Keep the cards you've yet to visit behind this divider. They are kept in numerical order so that you can easily find them when planning your visits for new studies.

Some of your cards will represent people who are more likely to take studies than others. Since you may not actually call upon all the cards, you want to put the most likely candidates for studies at the top of your visitation list. People who have already completed Bible studies with a media ministry usually turn out to be your best interests. Even those who enrolled in a course but didn't complete it are excellent prospects. I always make sure I get to these people before any of the others since they often offer a receptive welcome.

Another way to organize the church for giving studies is to divide your church's territory into sections. Appoint teams to be responsible for each area of your town. Any media responses, church visitors or other names that come to the church are given to the teams.

Taking the time to get organized is working in harmony with heaven and will help you be efficient. "God is a God of order. Everything connected with heaven is in perfect order; subjection and thorough discipline mark the movements of the angelic host. Success can only attend order and harmonious action." (*Patriarchs and Prophets*, p. 376).

Discuss, Learn, Apply

1. What are the advantages of having a partner with you to give Bible studies?

2. What do you have to especially pay attention to when you give Bible studies with a partner?

3. What do you have to pay attention to in regard to dress when you give Bible studies?

4. What ways do you see in your neighborhood to find people who are ready to take Bible studies?

Chapter 11
LEADING A PERSON TO CHRIST

I was giving a study on Jesus' soon return to a very nice Christian couple. I normally ask a salvation question at the end of this study, but all through the study, the thought kept nagging me that I didn't need to do this with this family. They had all the earmarks of converted Christians and I didn't want to insult them by questioning their salvation. At the end of the lesson, however, I took the plunge and asked them if they were ready to meet Jesus if He should return now or if they had the assurance of eternal life if they were to suddenly die. The husband thought for a long moment and then sincerely told me he believed he was ready. The wife, though, surprisingly dropped her head and gazed at the floor. I could tell something was desperately wrong and troubling her. She eventually broke the silence and somberly said, *"I don't think I'm ready."*

"Would you like to have the assurance of eternal life?" I sympathetically inquired. Thankfully, she said yes and I was able to share the gospel with her. We then bowed together in prayer and she gave her life to Jesus. When we rose from our knees she looked like a different person. She radiated a peace and confidence she didn't possess before.

Presenting the gospel is the most important thing we do. I never use my own judgment to determine whether I should ask if a person is ready for heaven, because I have found the devil is always nearby to suggest I not do it. In other areas, I may adapt to the particular situation, but when it comes to the gospel question, I always pose it. You also should not skip this vital point. It is one of the most exciting things you can do in your studies.

Every student should either make a favorable decision for Christ or reaffirm their commitment to Him before you introduce testing truths such as the Sabbath. So one of your first goals is to lead them to accept Jesus as Lord and Saviour.

The importance of doing this cannot be overemphasized. What difference does it make if you help someone become a Sabbath keeping, tithe-paying vegetarian if they have not surrendered to Jesus? Without this essential surrender our work for God is serving the purpose of Satan. Baptizing unconverted people successfully assists the enemy to infiltrate the camp of God with his most deceptive decoys. "Salvation is not to be baptized, not to have our names upon the church books, not to preach the truth. But it is a living union with Jesus Christ to be renewed in heart, doing the works of Christ in faith and labor of love, in patience, meekness, and hope. ... many join the church without first becoming united to Christ. In this Satan triumphs. Such converts are his most efficient agents. They serve as decoys to other souls" (*Evangelism*, p. 319, 320).

Pose the gospel question by the third or fourth study. You don't want to do this too early because you may not have established enough confidence for the person to open up to you. Most lesson series have a study on salvation and this is an idea time to ask for their decision.

Here is a sample dialogue I often use to lead a person to Christ:

"John, today we learned Jesus will soon return to earth to take His children home. I want to be ready for him, don't you? As we look at the provision God has made for us to live with Him in heaven, I wonder if I can ask you what may be a personal question. If you are uncomfortable answering it, you can just tell me. But when I study the Bible with someone, I feel this is the most important question we can answer. Do you want to hear the question? (Wait for their answer.) *Okay, here it is. If Jesus were to come back tonight or you were to die suddenly, are you assured you have eternal life?"*

If there is a long pause, you can say, *"I told you it was a heavy question."* Then you should wait while they ponder its significance. Embrace the silence and don't be afraid of it. Allow the Spirit to use the quiet to speak to your student's heart.

If they respond that they do have assurance of eternal life, then you will enthusiastically say:

"That's fantastic! Now, may I ask you another question? Say you go up to the pearly white gates of heaven, and before you enter, an angel stops you and says, 'John, we are so happy that you are here. We have been looking forward to your entrance into heaven for a long time. But before we let you in we need you to answer a question. Why should God let you enter?' John, how would you answer the angel's question?"

The correct answer is that they should be allowed to enter because of what Jesus did for them on the Cross, they have accepted Him as their Savior and have sought to follow Him as the Lord of their life.

If they respond by saying they will tell the angel they have tried to live a good life and have not been a bad person, then you will know they don't understand the gospel. Others will tell you, *"I don't know what I would say."*

Depending on their answer, you will say, *"I'm glad to hear that you're seeking to live a good life for God,"* or *"Thank you for your honesty. Most of us would probably be speechless in the face of such a question."* In either case, here is how you respond to anything but the correct answer:

"May I suggest an answer the Bible endorses? We can humbly confess to the angel, 'I am not worthy to enter heaven. But Jesus came to earth and lived a perfect life to die for me on the Cross. I have accepted Him as my Savior to forgive my sins and I followed Him as my Lord to tell me how to live. It has all been by His grace and this is why I should be allowed to enter.' Now isn't this a good answer? The emphasis is on what Jesus has done. We can't do anything to earn heaven. It is ours as a gift from God. But we are to surrender our life to Him so that we can be forgiven of our past sins and for the Holy Spirit to enable us to live in harmony with God's will."

Now you will ask, *"John, may I briefly review the reason this answer will be our best ticket into heaven?"* When they say, *"Yes,"* you will present the gospel. A sample gospel presentation is in the side bar. If you'd like to have a small tract that you can read with them, you can use *The Four Spiritual Laws* tract mentioned earlier.

Four Universal Truths

(Make this presentation simple by using only the texts in italics.)

1. God loves you and created you to know peace and happiness (Jeremiah 29:11; *John 3:16; 10:10*). So why don't people experience the abundant life full of inner peace and happiness?

2. Because we are sinful and our sins have separated us from the abundant life God designed us for (*Romans 3:23*; Isaiah 59:2). When Adam and Eve chose to use their will to rebel against God's plan they immediately became selfish by nature and passed this selfish nature to us (Genesis 3:12; Romans 5:12; 3:10). This is why we cannot enjoy the peace of God without a power to change our selfish natures. This power is revealed in the third universal truth.

3. God's Son, Jesus Christ, came and lived as a man to break the power of sin and selfishness in our natures. He showed us what

the love of God really is like so we can be brought back to God to experience His power and love in our lives (*Hebrews 2:14, 15*; Romans 5:8). Knowing these three universal truths is not sufficient. We must also have the fourth universal truth if we are to find the assurance of eternal life and peace.

4. We need to personally ask Jesus to forgive our sins and to live in our life. Then we will experience the plans God has for us, not only in this earth, but in heaven as well (*Acts 16:30, 31; 2:37, 38*; John 3:7; John 1:12; Ephesians 2:8, 9). We must choose to repent of our sins and give our life to Jesus and then we can know that we have the assurance of a new life with Christ.

These are the four universal truths. Now let me ask you a question. Of the following two descriptions which one best describes your life right now? (Answer "a.")

a. You are living your own life by your own wisdom and thoughts and your life is experiencing conflict and lack of peace.

b. Jesus is directing your life and giving you wisdom to make the right choices and He is giving you power and victory.

Which one would you like to describe your life? (Answer "b.")

You can have Jesus forgive your past sins and mistakes and come into your life and give you eternal life. All you need to do is ask Him (*Matthew 7:7; 1 John 5:11–15*).

Would you like for me to lead you in a prayer so that you can have the assurance that Jesus Christ is your Saviour and Lord?

(Lead the person in a prayer of FAITH.)

If in answer to your initial question, your student says they are not ready to meet Jesus should He come tonight or they die suddenly, you will respond with, *"Thank you for being so honest. I really appreciate this about you. Do you want to have the assurance that you are ready?"*

Usually, their answer will be positive. Then you offer, *"May I explain to you how you can have this assurance?"* If they give you permission, you will share a gospel presentation like mentioned above.

No matter how your student answers the questions you will want to end by leading them in a prayer committing their life to Christ or reaffirming their faith. If you can have them pray in their own words it will help. Otherwise, they can repeat after you in prayer. You should conclude with your own prayer thanking God for the gift of Jesus and the eternal life

He gives us. Thank Him for your student and the decision they've made for Christ.

Prayer of FAITH

Here is a simple prayer of surrender that you can lead a person to repeat after you. You can recall the prayer's five parts by remembering FAITH (James 5:15).

F Forgive me "Jesus, I ask You to Forgive me of my sins."

A Accept my confession "Please Accept my confession that I am a sinner worthy of death."

I I give my life "I now give my life completely to you."

T Thank you "Thank you for the free gift of salvation that is now mine by faith in Jesus' death and life."

H Help me to walk in your ways "Now, Help me to walk in all Your ways by Your grace and power."

Discuss, Learn, Apply

1. Why is it important to stress a personal relationship with Jesus?

2. Which question can we ask to find out if someone has assurance of salvation?

3. What do you say if a person says they do have assurance of salvation?

4. What do you say if they do not have assurance of salvation?

5. How do you explain in four simple steps how somebody can accept Jesus as their Savior?

Chapter 12
HOW TO GIVE YOUR TESTIMONY

I once missed an excellent chance to share my testimony. My airplane was delayed in a small city in northern Alabama due to mechanical problems. Since it was time for lunch, the airline gave all the passengers meal vouchers to use at the small airport restaurant. With just a few tables available and a plane full of hungry passengers, a number of us ended up eating together. At our table we went around and shared who we were and what we did for a living. When it came my turn, I told the group I was a minister. This always brings a variety of interesting responses but I was unprepared for what the young professional tennis player next to me asked. He wondered what I was before becoming a Christian. Even years later I still cringe when I think about what I said next. Instead of seeing this as an opportunity to share my testimony, I brashly announced, *"I was a pagan."* I should have known I had really missed the mark when he quizzically responded, *"What is a pagan?"* Still completely out of touch, I went on to tell of my non-Christian background in the most unflattering terms. Looking back, I now realize I was inadvertently describing this young man's lifestyle. Eventually it dawned on me what had happened, but it was too late for me to recover the can of worms I had opened.

Later that day the Lord gave me another chance. When our flight resumed, I sat next to a former member of our church. He told me many things during our several-hour flight but he really surprised me when he confessed, *"I am serving money."* This was no ignorant, uncultured man sitting next to me. Nor was this an uncalculated decision that he had stumbled into. This was a deliberate decision he made as a young man. He explained that he was working on a law degree so that he could live on the legal edge and become wealthy. Now here was someone I could witness to. God gave me words to speak that captured his attention. He listened intently as I described how I had found Jesus to be the real answer for lasting happiness.

There is nothing as influential to convert others than our own testimony of what God has done for us. "As witnesses for Christ, we are to tell what we know, what we ourselves have seen and heard and felt. ... We can tell how we have tested His promise, and found the promise true. We can bear witness to what we have known of the grace of Christ. This is the witness for which our Lord calls, and for want of which the world is perishing" (*The Desire of Ages*, p. 340).

It's a good practice to write down your testimony. This will help you hear how it may sound to others. Do not use religious clichés such as "*Since I came into the message;*" "*after I accepted the truth;*" or "*when I learned the truth of the Sabbath.*" Keep it focused on Christ and the plan of salvation. Uplift Jesus with phrases such as "*Since I accepted Christ,*" and "*After I accepted Jesus as my Saviour.*" Do not glamorize sin by telling the details of how sinful you used to be or speak critically of other churches. You also want to keep it brief.

People who were raised as Christians may lament they don't have a testimony. We don't have to be scraped from the bottom of society to have a testimony that will inspire others. "Conversions are not all alike. Jesus impresses the heart, and the sinner is born again to new life. Often souls have been drawn to Christ when there was no violent conviction, no soul rending, no remorseful terrors. They looked upon an uplifted Saviour; they lived. They saw the soul's need; they saw the Saviour's sufficiency and His claims; they heard His voice saying, 'Follow Me,' and they rose up and followed Him. This conversion was genuine, and the religious life was just as decided as was that of others who suffered all the agony of a violent process" (*Evangelism*, p. 287, 288).

If you were converted as a young person, remember it is not a badge of honor to have been scarred by sin. Thank the Lord for the truth you were blessed to be raised with and for the God you learned to love and trust as a child.

Now practice your personal testimony until it becomes natural. Here is a thrilling assignment. Ask God to make you aware of someone who needs to hear your testimony. Keep alert. He will show you the person. When you sense the Spirit impressing you, present your personal testimony with a radiant smile.

Here is an outline for your testimony.

MY LIFE BEFORE I ACCEPTED CHRIST
  "I needed help" (*Testimonies for the Church*, Vol. 8, p. 321).
HOW I BECAME A CHRISTIAN
  "I found it in Jesus. Every want was supplied, the hunger of my soul was satisfied; and the Bible is to me the revelation of Christ" (*ibid*).
MY LIFE SINCE BECOMING A CHRISTIAN (tell of the change, the joy, and blessings)
  "I believe the Bible because I have found it to be the voice of God to my soul" (*ibid*).

Discuss, Learn, Apply

Please write down your personal testimony in three steps.

1. My life before I knew Jesus
2. How I became a Christian
3. My life as a Christian

Chapter 13
STUDIES ON STEROIDS

I was giving studies to a man who had a passion for refereeing ball games. Of course these games were on Sabbath mornings. I knew the Sabbath was going to be a special test for him. Early in our studies I privately began to pray a special prayer during my early morning devotions. *"Lord, you know how much Ralph enjoys refereeing games and how these games are on Sabbath. I ask that you give Ralph a love for You and Your truth that supersedes his love for this sport."*

Shortly after presenting the Sabbath lesson to Ralph, I walked into church one Sabbath morning. As I was going down the center aisle, I heard someone repeatedly hissing, *"Psst! Psst!"* Along with half the church, I turned to see Ralph sitting in a pew and frantically waving at me in as reverent a fashion as he could muster. I went over and welcomed him to church. With a broad smile on his face, he proudly announced, *"Gary, this is my first Sabbath. You know how much I love refereeing. The national playoffs will soon begin and I've been asked to be one of the referees. Guess when the practice is being held? It's today. But look at me. I am here in God's house!"*

Then Ralph told me something that still sends chills up my spine. *"Gary, I really wanted to officiate at the nationals. It has been a dream of mine and it would be a great honor. As I was debating what to do, it was like God spoke to me. It wasn't audible, but I heard his voice in my heart nonetheless. God said, 'Ralph, what is it going to be? Sports or Me? Do you love me more than you love your sport?' Gary, I told God that I love Him most of all and that I would give up the sport to follow Him. This is why I am here this Sabbath and not out on the ball field."*

You can present the most fabulous studies in the world and not convert anyone. To really be successful you need to give "studies on steroids." They must be power packed with the Holy Spirit if you are going to change lives. Even proper witnessing methods cannot accomplish this supernatural transformation. The Holy Spirit alone can give you ability to impress hearts to trust and obey Jesus.

"One might be able to present the letter of the Word of God, he might be familiar with all its commands and promises; but unless the Holy Spirit sets home the truth, no souls will fall on the Rock and be broken. No amount of education, no advantages, however great, can make one a channel of light without the cooperation of the Spirit of God. The sowing of the gospel seed will not be a success unless the seed is quickened into life by the dew of heaven" (*The Desire of Ages*, p. 672).

As you approach the time to present a testing truth, pray for God to prepare your student's heart to receive it. Ask Him for wisdom on how to present the message to this unique person. The Lord will give you insight into their life and what really motivates them to make right decisions. Use their motivation to inspire them to follow Christ.

The Holy Spirit can do things for people we can't. So pray, pray, pray. For extra encouragement read the following statements often to remind yourself of what the Spirit will do when you seek Him.

Pray for Your Students

"In times past there were those who fastened their minds upon one soul after another, saying, 'Lord, help me to save this soul.' But now such instances are rare. How many act as if they realized the peril of sinners? How many take those whom they know to be in peril, presenting them to God in prayer, and supplicating Him to save them?" (*Gospel Workers*, p. 65).

"Through much prayer you must labor for souls, for this is the only method by which you can reach hearts" (*Evangelism*, p. 342).

"Begin to pray for souls; come near to Christ ... and let your earnest, broken, humble petitions ascend to Him for wisdom that you may have success in saving not only your own soul, but the souls of others" (*Testimonies for the Church*, Vol. 1, p. 513).

The Need of the Spirit

"Unless the Spirit of God sets the truth home, the character will not be transformed. Without the enlightenment of the Spirit, men will not be able to distinguish truth from error, and they will fall under the masterful temptations of Satan" (*Christ's Object Lessons*, p. 408, 409).

"The work of the Holy Spirit is immeasurably great. It is from this source that power and efficiency come to the worker for God" (*Gospel Workers*, p. 289).

The Need of Prayer

"The Holy Spirit will come to all who are begging for the bread of life to give to their neighbors" (*Testimonies for the Church*, Vol. 6, p. 90).

"God's faithful messengers are to seek to carry forward the Lord's work in His appointed way ... They are to wrestle with God in earnest prayer for a baptism of the Holy Spirit that they may meet the needs of a world perishing in sin. All power is promised those who go forth in faith to proclaim the everlasting gospel" (*Testimonies to Ministers*, p. 459).

"Morning by morning, as the heralds of the gospel kneel before the Lord and renew their vows of consecration to Him, He will grant them the presence of His Spirit, with its reviving, sanctifying power. As they go forth to the day's duties, they have the assurance that the unseen agency of the Holy Spirit enables them to be laborers together with God" (*The Acts of the Apostles*, p. 56).

"Ask Him for the gift of the Holy Spirit. The Lord wants us to trouble Him in this matter. He wants us to press our petitions to the throne" (*Fundamentals of Christian Education*, p. 537).

"A close connection with heaven will give the right tone to your fidelity and will be the ground of your success. Your feeling of dependence will drive you to prayer and your sense of duty summon you to effort. Prayer and effort, effort and prayer, will be the business of your life. You must pray as though the efficiency and praise were all due to God, and labor as though duty were all your own. If you want power you may have it, as it is waiting your draft upon it. Only believe in God, take Him at His word, act by faith, and blessings will come" (*Counsels on Health*, p. 367).

"You can do more than pray after you have prayed, but you can never do more than pray until you have prayed." A. J. Gordon. (Author Unknown, quoted in *The Kneeling Christian*. Zondervan Publishing House. Grand Rapids, MI 49506. Copyright 1971.)

Cooperating With the Spirit

"The Lord requires the human agent not to move by impulse in speaking, but to move calmly, speak slowly, and let the Holy Spirit give efficiency to the truth" (*Evangelism*, p. 668).

Discuss, Learn, Apply

1. What can the best outreach methods not accomplish?

2. Please describe the sources of power in sharing the gospel.

3. Please read again Ellen White's statements in this chapter and write down the passages that appeal to you most.

4. In the light of this chapter, what do you want to put into practice?

Chapter 14
Sit-Down or Drop-Off?

*T*here are several different methods for giving studies. Most used is the drop-off study. This is where a study guide is left with a student to read and answer the questions. One week later the Bible instructor returns to correct the lesson and leave the next in the series. Drop-off studies can include video or audio tapes of evangelistic sermons. This is a very easy method to utilize and only involves your ability to befriend the person and to correct their lessons. It is preferred that you set an appointment to visit the student every week to exchange the lessons. This will give you the chance to talk and get acquainted. You will ask the student if they have any questions from the lesson. If they do, you will answer them from the Bible. Over time, you want to win the student's confidence and have the opportunity to help them make a choice to follow Christ.

A second method is the sit-down study. With this the Bible instructor actually studies the lesson with the student. Some people prefer to use their sit-down study to review the study guide question by question with the person. The instructor makes appropriate comments about each question and checks to see they wrote the correct answers.

Another way is for the instructor to present a study directly from the Bible without the use of the study guide. In this situation, both the instructor and student open their Bibles and read the texts as the instructor guides them through the topic. The student is encouraged to have a notebook for taking notes.

The study guide is then given as a summary of the presentation for them to complete during the week. At the next appointment the instructor quickly scans the study guide and asks if they have any questions. Then they present the next sit-down study with Bibles open. Again, a study guide is given as a review of the presentation.

The method you choose largely depends upon your comfort level with giving studies. The sit-down study is more challenging for most people to do. To make it very easy to do a sit-down study, I have written the book *Winsome Studies in Prophecy, Dynamic Bible Studies You Can Give!* This is a series of Bible study scripts that tells you exactly what to say in a study. It is very easy to use and goes along with the *Prophecies of Hope* Bible study guides that I recommend you leave with your students. In some editions of *Winsome Witnessing*, you will find a copy of *Winsome Studies* included on a CD. If not, you can contact the author to get a copy.

Before you choose which method to use, let's look at some of the positives and negatives of each approach. More people are willing to take drop-off studies because it is less threatening to do. This should not be construed to mean more people would be baptized, since more drop-off study students tend to quit taking the lessons.

One of the downsides to drop-off studies is that it doesn't qualify your students. Since it doesn't require much commitment to accept the study offer, many people will allow you to leave the lessons at their home, but they are not serious. They don't complete the studies, aren't home when you bring their lessons and are unwilling to allow you to develop relationships.

Sit-down studies generally attract a more likely convert. Their openness to have you visit in their home for one hour each week to study the Bible demonstrates they're receptive to new ideas. It also reveals their willingness to develop a friendship with you. This often translates into a higher percentage of converts.

Another benefit to the sit-down study is that it helps the instructor learn their Bible better and develops communication skills for explaining the Bible. If these are some of your personal goals, then you will definitely want to focus on the sit-down method.

Occasionally, I meet a person who is very interested but they refuse the sit-down study. After unsuccessfully trying to remove their objections, I will revert to offering them drop-off studies. For people who aren't receptive to this, I will offer a study series through the mail. I usually send their names to one of the many good correspondence courses offered by our media ministries.

I prefer to do the vast majority of my studies as sit-downs. Those who invite me into their home to teach the Bible do not quit the lessons as frequently as the drop-off students. And the close relationships we develop enable me to help them accept the life changing truths they learn. For this reason, I choose not to do any drop-off studies. I've learned I can keep more than busy with the vast number of persons who willingly invite me into their homes. I don't need to spend my time chasing down people who are only marginally interested.

Having revealed my preference for sit-down studies, I hasten to add you *can* do the drop-off studies effectively. To accomplish this, you need to have a strategy to develop a relationship with your student. "You must come close to those for whom you labor, that they may not only hear your voice, but shake your hand, learn your principles, feel your sympathy" (*Gospel*

Workers, p. 192). The best way to do this is to find a point in the relationship that you can gradually transition the drop-off student into a sit-down study. This may start with you socializing as you drop their lessons by. Then it can progress to answering any questions they may raise. Eventually you will offer to personally study a topic with them in which they seem especially interested. This can then turn into a regular sit-down study.

Some instructors combine drop-off studies with small neighborhood group studies. This works better in some cultures than others. After a relationship has been established, students taking drop-off studies are invited to a home group for an interesting study on a topic designed to draw them to the new setting. Good topics for this first meeting include the second coming of Jesus and other prophetic topics. While the subjects need to have a high interest value, you don't want to be so controversial that you shock them before establishing confidence. If you cover topics like the beast, you can be less specific at first.

When doing a sit-down study, you will first present the lesson from your Bible and then you'll leave the study guide as a review of the topic you've just covered. One reason this works best is that you are able to use your personality to influence the student favorably for the subject. For example, when presenting the Sabbath you are able to look into your student's eyes and smile, and use the pleasant tones of your voice to communicate that the Sabbath is a welcome blessing from God. This makes it far easier for them to accept because it breaks down prejudice and puts a pleasant face on what is often a startling teaching.

On the other hand, if you choose to allow the student to read and complete the study guide before you actually present the lesson, you may find that prejudices are aroused. Let me give you an example of how this can play out.

Let's say you are giving studies to a lady who is active in her church. All your studies leading up to the Sabbath have been positive experiences. You leave her the Sabbath lesson to complete and tell her you will study it together at your next appointment. During the week she reads it and is surprised by this teaching. She remembers hearing her minister preach on the Sabbath. He said it was part of the Old Covenant. She calls a respected elder at her church and tells him she has some questions. Her elder alerts the pastor. The two of them present her with anti-sabbatarian literature and malign your church. When you return to present your study, you find your once-receptive student has closed her mind. She bombards you with questions that are asked more as a challenge and less from a sincere heart that wants to know truth.

This situation can be easily avoided by giving the study guide *after* you have presented the lesson. This allows you the first opportunity to process with your student any shock the topic might cause. Then they are less likely to feel the need to go to someone else. Of course, different personality types relate in a variety of ways. But the method we've just described is the safest for the largest group of persons with whom you'll work.

When presenting a sit-down study, it is entirely appropriate to use some notes to help you remember which texts you'll cover and the points you'll make. I like to have my *Winsome Studies in Prophecy* notes printed on half pages I place next to my Bible. This allows me to see at a quick glance the points I need to make and gives me freedom to change and adapt the study over time as my experience grows. (You can do the same thing with the *Winsome Studies* in prophecy notes on the data CD included with this book. The studies are in a format that you can even edit them to fit your needs.)

Sit-down studies are especially easy to obtain with people who have previously taken a correspondence course. The following dialogue is a sample approach to use to get these people to agree to in-the-home studies with you. (For a more complete canvass on how to get people to commit to doing a sit-down study, please consult the *Something Wonderful For You Card Canvass* in the appendix.)

"Jane, how did you enjoy the course you took through the mail? (Discuss what they liked about the correspondence lessons.) *Jane, we have an advanced course I think you will really like. These guides cover ...* (Show a sample copy of the first lesson or two and explain why they are so interesting. Usually, a course on Bible prophecy will be the most effective in getting the person to commit.) *The best thing about the advance series is it includes personal instruction. With the correspondence course you probably wished at times for someone to talk to about the lessons.* (Really build this point and talk about how long it takes to receive lessons in the mail and how this increases the time it takes to finish a course. Many people lose interest and never achieve their goal.) *The advanced course eliminates the weaknesses of the correspondence course and it provides a 'live person' you can ask questions. The way the program works is this: I come by once a week and we open our Bibles and study together for about 30 to 45 minutes. Then I will give you a study guide that corresponds with what we just studied. People find they gain so much more from this method because they've heard the Bible*

study and then have the study guide as a review. The next week I will
return to answer any questions you might have. Then we will open
our Bibles to study the next topic. People really like this method and
get so much out of it. How does this sound to you? Is this a good time
for me to come back next week?"

Try both the sit-down and the drop-off methods of giving studies until you discover which is best for you. The important thing is to get started and see where the Lord leads you. He will use whichever method we choose. An exciting experience is in store for those who open the Bible to others.

Regardless which method you choose, don't think that because you leave lessons in a home your student will read their way into the remnant church. While this works with some people, it doesn't with the majority. We need to remember that we are in a war with Satan. He will do all he can to distract them.

As your student is introduced to unfamiliar testing truth it is your responsibility to give personal attention to them at this critical moment. If you are unavailable to answer questions and inspire confidence, the devil will provide his own counselors in the form of friends and family to confuse and discourage them. This point is important. "Many a laborer fails in his work because he does not come close to those who most need his help" (*Gospel Workers*, p. 190).

It requires less sacrifice from us to simply drop lessons at a person's home. As soon as we engage in a person's life and seek to influence them for Christ, it costs us something. To win people you must be willing to sacrifice time, effort and love of ease. "Souls cannot be saved without exertion" (*Gospel Workers*, p. 196).

When we look at Calvary we understand the infinite price God paid to save us. Should we be willing to give any less for others? When we sacrifice our comfort we are rewarded with richer insights into what God has done for us. These revelations of God's love are worth all the sacrifice we make, for they cannot be obtained in any other way than through actual labor. Jesus gave all He had to save our souls. He now calls us to follow in His steps.

Discuss, Learn, Apply

1. Please name and briefly describe the different methods of giving Bible studies mentioned in this chapter. What are the advantages and disadvantages of each of these methods?

Chapter 15
WHICH STUDIES SHOULD I USE?

O ne of my early students was an airline pilot who was a committed Christian. I was pretty pleased to get a study with a professional of his caliber. At our initial meeting, I left the first two lessons for him to do and made an appointment to pick them up the next week. When I returned, my enthusiasm wilted as he told me he wasn't interested any longer. He explained he knew everything in the guides and that he was looking for something more insightful.

Saying a quick prayer in my heart I ventured into what was then new territory for me. *"You know, I have something that I've recently been studying that I think you would find interesting. It's on Bible prophecy. Would you like to hear about it?"* His curiosity aroused, he invited me into his house, where we sat and studied the Bible for an hour. At the end of my presentation, I did something I learned while growing up watching television. In my era many of the children's shows such as Batman ended with what is know as cliffhangers. At a high point in the action and drama the program would suddenly freeze the frame as the announcer's voice dramatically intoned, *"Stay tuned next time to discover if the villain finally gets to win this one."* Cliffhangers were effective ways to get you back in front of the boob tube for the next broadcast. At the conclusion of our study, I teased the pilot, *"It looks like we are out of time and I have to get to my next appointment. (I really did.) We don't have time to get into which prophecy Jesus presented to His disciples that convinced them He was the Messiah, but if you'd like, we can get back together next week and continue."* *"O, no! Are you sure you can't stay?"* The pilot swallowed my bait. As I slowly shook my head, he said, *"Well then, I'll see you next week."* We went on to have studies that were some of the most filled with the presence of God's Spirit that I have ever given. I was thankful God gave this novice Bible instructor the words to say that day. From this early experience I learned a very important principle.

The order of topics and the study guides you use has a lot to do with your level of success. Most lessons assume you are studying with a person who has little or no knowledge of the Bible. This is one reason they start with the authority of the Scriptures and other elementary subjects. While these early lessons are appropriate for non-Christians or new believers, they can prove too simple for many others.

It is vital to keep a high level of interest in the studies from the very beginning. To accomplish this you need an order of topics that explains Scriptures not previously understood by your student. Basic Bible studies are fine for a non-Christian, but most believers will be more attracted by Bible prophecy. A Bible instructor told me of a very interested group of committed Christian women she was studying with. They told her that they were considering the need to quit their studies. The Bible instructor asked me what she should do. I suggested she switch to a prophecy series. She told me later that her students absolutely loved the lessons and didn't talk about stopping anymore.

At the end of this chapter is the order of topics I use in my *Prophecies of Hope* study guides with great success. This simple presentation of truth in a prophetic context is extremely convincing and eliminates virtually all of the typical objections to the Sabbath and other Bible doctrines. I wrote these lessons with the specific goal of helping you be successful in giving studies by including a host of phrases and techniques not found in any other lessons. Consequently, lay people and evangelists using the *Prophecies of Hope* lessons say they are the most effective lessons they've used. Ordering information for *Prophecies of Hope* can be found on the back page. And remember, the *Winsome Studies in Prophecy* Bible instructor's scripts that I authored will tell you exactly what to say as you present each lesson in the home. The complete package will help you succeed in leading people to Christ.

To begin, choose one or two sets of studies and stick with them. Start at the beginning of the series and work through each lesson with your student. There are occasions where you may skip a lesson or reorder them a little more to your liking and to match them to your students' spiritual maturity.

One lesson ought to build on the other and the student must have time to gain confidence in you as an instructor, in the reliability of the lessons and in the message. Every lesson series seeks to accomplish this through a progressive order. I met one Bible instructor who never knew what they were going to present in their next study because they were allowing the student to pick the topics out of thin air. It is no mystery why their students never made decisions. You want to stay with the order of the studies and you don't want to allow the student to choose which topics you will be covering.

The exception to this is when something in the series will not build confidence and credibility if presented in the order given. Many years ago there was a set of lessons that presented the seventy weeks of Daniel

9 in the second study. This was premature for most students. They either found it complex or felt their entire belief system was threatened. People lost confidence in the lessons and the instructor and stopped studying. When I used this series, I skipped this lesson and put it later when most people would more readily accept it.

I was thrilled to begin studies with the popular anchorman of a television evening news program that reached nearly half the state. This was an unprecedented breakthrough for our little church. I was impressed during my visit with the anchorman that he was a committed Christian who had done quite a bit of biblical research. He was especially interested in our lessons because he was intrigued by prophecy. I met the anchorman while an intern pastor and I were visiting people who had sent cards to our church requesting study guides. This was part of the new pastor's training and I was helping him learn how I give studies. Since I lived a hundred miles away, this was going to be one the capable intern would do on his own.

During this time I was using the lessons that taught the seventy-weeks prophecy in the second study guide. This especially concerned me with the anchorman because all evangelical interpretations of prophecy depend heavily on an incorrect view of the seventieth week. Any well-versed evangelical like him would immediately spot the implications of our study guide's different interpretation and realize it undermines everything they believe to be true about last-day events. I was concerned we could lose this particular student over covering this topic so early. After leaving the anchorman's house, I instructed the intern to skip the second lesson with the seventy-weeks prophecy in it and explained the reasons for doing this.

Several weeks later I discovered the anchorman was no longer studying with us. I was devastated. He was a promising person who could do a lot for God's cause in our area and I wanted a chance to get him into the deeper truths of Scripture. When I inquired why he quit, my associate confessed he had not heeded my advice and had presented the seventy-week lesson in the second study. Unfortunately, all my concerns materialized as the anchorman raised multiple questions about our interpretation. After the study he told the intern he could not except our view and requested he not return. It would have been much better to gradually build toward this challenging topic until confidence was developed. Some lessons are learned the hard way and God's grace is sufficient in every situation. The moral of the story is be careful of the order of your lessons and follow a path that allows time to develop confidence in your material and you as a teacher of truth.

To determine which studies to use, we should first make a distinction between the two types available. Most study guides are topical—each lesson in the series covers a separate topic. The lessons are arranged in an order that prepares the student to accept the life-changing teachings of the Bible. Foundational doctrines of salvation, inspiration of Scriptures and the relationship between law and grace are taught before the Sabbath, death, health and other testing truths. The connection between the studies is not intimate and each topic essentially stands alone. Examples of topical studies include the *Amazing Facts Study Guides, Storacles of Prophecy* and *Discover Lessons.*

The second category of studies is the thematic study. These contain a connected theme, story or book of the Bible throughout the series. While thematic studies also cover individual topics, each lesson is interconnected by way of the common theme. A good example of thematic studies are my *Prophecies of Hope* lessons. These cover the entire message in the context of prophecy. Various Revelation and Daniel seminars are other examples.

Of these two types of studies, which should you use? The answer depends partly upon your preference and upon your student. I personally favor prophecy studies. I find it prepares a person better for testing truth. This is especially true of my *Prophecies of Hope* study guides. In my lessons, the Sabbath is presented in the setting of the great controversy as the focal point in the war between Christ and Satan. This type of presentation fills the Sabbath with conviction that is powerful to change lives.

It also circumvents most of the arguments people use against the Sabbath. If a non-believer accepts the identity of the little horn of Daniel 7, then it is an easy bridge to help them see this power readily admits to changing the sanctity of God's seventh-day Sabbath to the first day of the week. They find no reason to dispute whether we need to keep the law for salvation if they've already agreed the antichrist's strategy is to "think to change times and laws" (Daniel 7:25).

If you've never used prophecy lessons before, or are just starting, I want to encourage you to try the *Prophecies of Hope* lessons advertised on the back page. Combined with the *Winsome Studies in Prophecy* instructor's notes, you will find a new ease and confidence when giving studies. You will also experience how prophecy enables your students to truly understand God's message for this day and feel the Spirit's conviction to make a decision.

The most important thing about which studies you use is that you are comfortable and enthusiastic about sharing them. There are a large variety of electronic studies that are especially good. Videos and DVDs are very popular and effective. If you are using a video or DVD series you will want to try to match the personality and style of the speaker with that of the person you're studying with. You will find your student will show much more interest in the study if they can relate to the teacher.

Begin by experimenting with a variety of types of studies until you find one that you are especially effective with.

Order of Topics for Bible Studies

Title	Description
1. Our Day in Bible Prophecy (Daniel 2)	Prophecy tells us the end is near!
2. The Mark of the Beast Issue (Daniel 3)	The Bible's nine clues to the mark excite people to study. (This lesson doesn't reveal the mark.)
3. Bible Secrets to Personal Peace (Daniel 4)	The secret to real happiness is in the gospel.
4. Prophecy's Super Powers (Daniel 7)	A tactful study on the identity of the little horn.
5. A Bold Attack On God (Daniel 8)	The attempt by the devil to destroy God's Church.
6. The Bible's Most Important Prophecy (Daniel 9)	The New Testament comes to life in the 70 weeks prophecy.
7. The Longest Time Prophecy (2300 Days)	A dynamic revelation of the 2300 day prophecy.
8. God's Great Judgment (Judgment)	The good news of the judgment that began in 1844 prepares for the Sabbath study.
9. Satan's Secret Strategy (Law and Grace)	The strategy to "think to change times and laws" is exposed.
10. Prophecy's Day of Hope (Sabbath)	A Christ-centered and irrefutable study identifying the true Sabbath.

Title	Description
11. The Missing Text (Sunday Texts)	Bible answers to the change of the Sabbath.
12. Power for Living (Daniel 6)	How to live for God in the last days.
13. Revelation's Glorious Rapture (Second Coming)	The real truth about the rapture.
14. Death's Mystery Solved (Death)	What happens when a person dies?
15. Prophecy's 1,000 Years of Peace (Millennium)	What happens in the millennium?
16. The Truth About Hell (Hell)	The final fate of the lost.
17. Fit for the End Time (Health)	Bible insights to optimum health.
18. Door To A New Life (Baptism)	Baptism is the door to a new life of joy.
19. The Abomination of Desolation	Learn how Sabbath-breaking is the sign of the end.
20. Mark of the Beast	The mark of the beast and God's seal.
21. America in Prophecy	The USA's role in last day events.
22. Revelation's Two Women (Remnant Church)	God's last day church is revealed in prophecy.
23. Cleansed From the Inside Out (Christian Lifestyle)	How to live a successful Christian life.
24. Modern Prophets (Spirit of Prophecy)	How to identify true and false prophets.
25. The Unpardonable Sin	How not to commit this sin.
26. What Will Heaven Really Be Like? (Heaven)	An exciting look at our future home.

Discuss, Learn, Apply

1. Please write down some study topics that are well suited for beginners.

2. Now write down some topics that work well for people who already have some biblical knowledge.

3. Name and describe the two kinds of Bible study material that are mentioned in this chapter. Which of the two do you prefer? Explain.

Chapter 16
ANSWERING DIFFICULT QUESTIONS

M y very first student was a walking encyclopedia of Bible questions. Every week he brought out a notebook page full of them. I felt the Lord was baptizing me by fire. Early on he asked me a question on baptism that completely stumped me. Even though I didn't have the foggiest clue to the answer, I wasn't unnerved. What I did was show him how to use a concordance to find the answer in his own Bible. I loaned him a concordance (I carried extras in my car) and demonstrated how to find all the New Testament texts related to baptism. I instructed him to write these texts down and beside each one note what that text says about this subject. After assembling all these key points he should have a good idea about the answer to his question. I never told him that I didn't know the answer and he was none the wiser to my ignorance.

Meanwhile, I went home to study the topic for myself. When I returned the following week, he had several pages of texts and summary points he had written. When I saw all of his notes, I thought that at the very least this exercise kept him occupied and from conjuring up more questions. But then he shared his research with me and I realized I didn't even need to convey my information. He had discovered the truth for himself! This is a superb way to help people find answers. The genius of this approach is there is no need to try to convince them of the truth. They are persuaded because they found it through their own Spirit-led study.

If there is one thing every new Bible instructor fears more than anything else, it is the difficult questions. The good news is that you don't have to know all the answers. In this chapter you will learn several ways to turn perplexing questions into winning opportunities.

The first thing to do with any question is to affirm your student by saying, *"That's a very good question."* This will also give you time to evaluate whether you can answer it now or if it should be left to another time. Questions that are going to be covered in upcoming lessons should be deferred. For these you can say, *"We are going to have a whole lesson on this subject a little later. If you don't mind, can we discuss it more thoroughly at that time?"*

I like to bounce some questions back to the student with, *"That's a good question. What do you think about it?"* If after hearing their answer I think they need more study, I might say, *"That's good. Would you like an assignment that will help you find your answer? I can show you how to find it in your own Bible."* Then I will demonstrate how to use a concordance to look up key words. I'm always sure to explain that putting all the Bible texts together on a topic is how we understand what God teaches about any subject.

If you don't know the answer to a question, you can always confess, *"That's a good question. But to tell you the truth I've not thought about that one before. Give me a little time to research what the Bible has to say. OK?"* Sometimes you may have to point out, *"I think this is one of those questions where people have their opinions but the Bible doesn't clearly address it. We may have to wait for heaven for the answer."* Realize it isn't necessary for you to have something to say in response to every thought a person shares. It might be best to just nod your head and say, *"That's an interesting point,"* or *"I've not thought of it that way before."*

It is often wise not to directly correct most false statements made by your student. At least don't feel you have to correct them on the spot. Counter with, *"That is an interesting point. We have an entire study that will address it later."* Some people are so full of error that you may spend your entire lesson time correcting them. This will only serve to divert attention from your subject. Just remember Jesus lived with the disciples for three and a half years while they harbored false beliefs regarding the Messiah. This was the most critical doctrine of all time and it wasn't until the latter part of His earthly ministry that He directly countered their mistaken notions.

There are certain topics it is best to stay away from until you present the Sabbath or get them to attend an imminent evangelistic meeting. The secret rapture and speaking in tongues are two doctrines a lot of people get very emotional over. In one study, I had a lady who kept asking about my view of the rapture. I sensed she might be using this to determine whether she could trust me. One day she implored for what seemed like the hundredth time, *"Please tell me what you believe about the rapture. Are we going to be here during the tribulation or not? It doesn't matter what you say, we will still study together. I really want to know."*

Like Samson with Delilah, I fell for her persistent pleading. *"OK. I will tell you what the Bible says. It is very clear that we will go through the tribulation."* The lady immediately shot out of her seat and began ranting and raving. With her finger wagging in my face, she threatened, *"You may be here during the tribulation, but I'm not going to be!"* Soon she settled back down and we finished our study. She didn't keep her end of the bargain, however. The next week I found a note on her door telling me we would not be studying together any longer.

If I am going to lose a student over a controversial subject, I would rather lose them over the Sabbath more than anything else. The Sabbath is the testing truth for the last days. If I can at least present it, I know I've exposed them to a teaching they will encounter again when the loud cry is given under the power of the latter rain, if not before then. This is why I reserve some of these controversial subjects until after the Sabbath and related topics.

Whenever your student asks one of these really hot topics you want to be very careful about how and when you answer. When asked about the pre-tribulation rapture say, *"This is a question many Christians are divided over. One person has his opinion and another has hers. I have purposed in my studies not to confuse the issue any further by giving an opinion. What I will do for you is prepare a Bible study with all the relevant texts so you can read them. Then you can draw your own conclusion. Does this sound reasonable to you?"* After they tell you that they are interested in this study, you will say, *"Good. Let's plan to do it. But first I want to lay a foundation by looking at the events leading up to the rapture. This way it will make more sense when we study the rapture. So let's continue with the next several studies and then we will get to the rapture. OK?"* You will then continue with your order of topics just as you had planned all along.

Most students will allow you to do this. Don't fear that you are putting them off. They truly do need the background of the beast and other information before you can adequately answer the rapture question. Without this background, your study on the rapture will most likely just raise more questions and cause frustration.

For charismatic Christians, the subject of tongues is definitely a litmus test. They are taught that if they don't speak in tongues they aren't converted. This is why they want to know what you think. If I'm asked if I believe in the gift of tongues or the gifts of the Spirit I will answer, *"The Bible is very clear the gifts of the Spirit will be in the church until Jesus returns (1 Corinthians 1:7 and 1 Corinthians 12). The gift of tongues is definitely one of the spiritual gifts and it is active in God's church today. How about you? What do you think?"*

By answering in this manner you are not saying you believe the charismatics' manifestation of tongues is the true gift of the Spirit. This is not their question. I hope you do believe in the gift of tongues, because there is a true biblical gift. Whether or not the commonly practiced form meets the biblical criteria is another matter. It is best to leave this part of the issue for later.

Tongues is such a highly charged emotional issue that people caught by its spiritualistic grip have a hard time seeing the truth clearly. I always leave this study until the very last. Before we get to tongues, I want the student to accept the Bible's teaching on the Sabbath, death, hell, second coming, antichrist, sanctuary and all of the other important facets of the three angel's message. If accepted, these truths will do much to pry them away from the false gift. They ultimately will need to make a decision between rejecting the entire host of new truths they've learned to love or retaining a single belief in the counterfeit tongues. After having taken all of your studies, most people will begin to distrust what they've been taught about tongues and will give it up.

If someone asks an appropriate question for which you don't have a future study, and the answer means the difference in their obeying God, you can say, *"I see you have a serious question you want answered before you go any further on this topic. Would you like for me to prepare some material for your research for our next study?"*

Sometimes your student will repeat an objection they've heard someone else mention. Don't automatically assume they believe it. They might be curious how you will answer. It is important not to get defensive because this may cause the student to feel like they need to defend the objection. The best thing to do is to be quiet and listen to what they have to say. Ask how they answered the person bringing the objection or what they think about it. You will often find they will answer their own question and have already thought it through or defended the truth.

I discovered this while giving studies in St. Louis, Missouri. My student, Mr. White, had recently learned about the Sabbath and went to his pastor to ask why he did not teach the seventh-day Sabbath in their church. The pastor told him we are not under the old covenant and the Sabbath had been nailed to the cross. After Mr. White related the conversation he had with his pastor, I was tempted to answer the objections the pastor raised. The Holy Spirit prompted me instead to ask, *"What did you tell your pastor?"* Mr. White then described how he had answered every one of his pastor's objections with the correct Bible explanation. Mr. White consequently reinforced in his own mind the truths of the Bible.

If on, the other hand, I had countered the pastor's false theology, Mr. White might have been tempted to defend his pastor. This would tend to influence him to believe the erroneous teaching. "Men are influenced by their own words. Often under a momentary impulse, prompted by Satan, they give utterance to ... that which they do not really believe; but the expression reacts on the thoughts. They are deceived by their words, and come to believe that true which was spoken at Satan's instigation. Having once expressed an opinion or decision, they are often too proud to retract it, and try to prove themselves in the right, until they come to believe that they are" (*The Desire of Ages*, p. 323).

As far as possible, ask questions to discover what your student's views are before you launch into a defense of a doctrine. Remember you have twice as many ears as you do mouths. Therefore, listen twice as much as you talk. You may say, *"That's a great question. But I am curious why you ask it. What do you think about it?"* This will help you understand where the student is coming from and enable you to answer them in an appropriate fashion.

Some people are naturally argumentative. You need to evaluate if this is a character flaw or if it indicates they are not open to truth. If it is the latter, then you need to address their attitude directly and find out if it is worth your time to continue your studies. Say, *"Bob, I am happy to study with you, but it seems you don't really agree with much of what I present. Am I understanding you correctly?* (Listen to their answer.) *I am willing to continue studying together if you think it will help you learn more about the Bible, but I don't think arguing is profitable for either of us. How do you feel about this?"*

Jesus never entered into an argument. "The Saviour knew that no argument, however logical, would melt hard hearts or break through the crust of worldliness and selfishness" (*The Acts of the Apostles*, p. 31). Arguments never convert, but an antagonistic spirit can confirm a person in their error. "Argument, even when unanswerable, may provoke only opposition" (*The Acts of the Apostles*, p. 511). Don't try to back a person into a corner with your logic and be sure to keep the tone of your voice calm and respectful. "The spirit that is kept gentle under provocation will speak more effectively in favor of the truth than will any argument, however forcible" (*The Desire of Ages*, p. 353).

When arrested in the Jerusalem temple, the apostle Paul diffused the anger of his opponents by relating a personal experience. "Had he attempted to enter into argument with his opponents, they would have stubbornly refused to listen to his words; but the relation of his experience was attended with a convincing power that for the time seemed to soften and subdue their hearts" (*The Acts of the Apostles*, p. 409). You too can relieve a tense situation by sharing your experience or feelings in any of the following ways. *"There are many people who share your views. So I can understand what you are saying." "I know exactly how you feel. I have felt that way too." "I was brought up to believe this way too, so I can sympathize with you." "I respect your opinions. If you want I'll be happy to share with you why I believe as I do."*

There are times a student will confess that they can't accept what you are teaching. You want to try to relate to your student as much as possible by saying any of the following: *"You know, I asked the same questions when I was introduced to this subject. At first I couldn't believe it. But then, as I was praying about it, I realized that what I really wanted was Bible truth. That is when I decided that if this is what the Bible teaches and if it is what Jesus said, then it is what I want." "As we study to find God's will, I think the most important test for any teaching is, 'Is this what the Bible really teaches? Is there a clear 'thus saith the Lord' for what I currently believe?" "Is there any way I can help clarify what we have studied?" "I understand this subject may be different. May I share a pamphlet with you on this topic that you might find helpful?" "If I can explain what the Bible teaches any more clearly, I'll be glad to try."*

When answering questions and objections it is most important to be sincere and helpful. If you don't know the answer, seek to help them find it. Never argue. And most importantly always manifest a Christlike love and appreciation for your student. In the end it may be your love and practical Christianity that wins them more than your Bible knowledge because "a godly example has a power that it is impossible wholly to resist" (*The Acts of the Apostles*, p. 511).

Discuss, Learn, Apply

1. How can you answer questions regarding future topics in your Bible study series?

2. Sometimes it is good to ask a person what they think about their own question before answering. Why can this be good?

3. How do you respond when you don´t know the answer to a question?

4. What are two topics you may need to be especially cautious about? Why?

5. Why is it wise to listen twice as much as you talk when someone asks a question?

Chapter 17
TINY TYKES AND TV

Small children can be a major source of distraction to your study. They can be little angels all day, but as soon as company arrives and Bibles are opened, they sprout horns and do everything in their power to vie for attention. Before I had my own children, I entertained thoughts of carrying duct tape and a gag to take care of the little devils. Now I settle for suggesting a time to study when the dear ones are in bed, taking a nap or at school.

Having your partner entertain the bouncing balls of energy while you present the study is another option. This is not always welcomed by your partner but it does work. I once studied with a young family without the benefit of a co-worker. It was really difficult to keep them focused because their twenty-eight month old boy repeatedly raced through the living room leaving a path of destruction in his wake. The couch where I sat was smack in the middle of his runway. During the study I was startled to feel two little feet romp across my lap as I watched his diapered bottom scamper by. I was surprised his parents ever made a decision. This was one of the most challenging studies I ever conducted thanks to the little tyke. Since most parents will not welcome a stranger taking their children into another room alone, it is best if your partner entertains them in an adjacent, visible area with a coloring book or illustrated storybook.

There have been several occasions while giving studies that the phone constantly rang or people stopped by to visit at the most inconvenient time. The student would turn to me and say, *"I can't understand this. The phone doesn't ring all day, but when you get here it wont stop."* This is when you know the devil is trying to prevent them from concentrating. How can you handle the interruptions that are guaranteed to come?

I once knew a lady who left televisions on twenty-four hours a day in every room of her house including the bathroom. She could not endure the quiet. Some people are oblivious to the distraction a television can cause. If your student leaves theirs on during your study you can ask, *"Is this your favorite program?"* They will usually say *"No"* and turn it off. Another approach is to kindly suggest, *"Would it be okay to turn the television off?"* I've been known to request, *"May I turn the volume down?"* When they give me permission I reach for the remote and turn it really down. I switch it off.

One of the more disruptive interruptions is a neighbor or relative who happens to arrive during your study. In many instances this is a fantastic opportunity to invite them to join. Explain what you are doing and briefly review what you've discussed. Sometimes though the topic is too deep or it is a decision study that is not appropriate to do with a new person. In such delicate situations you can ask your student, *"Would you like to continue with the study now or would it be better for me to come back later?"*

There are many occasions when a gracious host will offer you coffee, tea, snacks, or meals that contain food items not appropriate for you to eat. While thanking them for their kind offer you can say, *"Thank you, but I ate very recently."* Try to avoid the issue of vegetarianism and clean and unclean foods. You don't want to bring this topic up prematurely. If you are asked *"May I get you something?"* respond with, *"Thank you very much. A glass of water would be perfect."*

One man insisted he entertain me for a barbecue in his back yard. Every week he pressed his invitation. I tried to avoid telling him I am a vegetarian because I didn't want to raise anything to divert our study. Finally, I had to address his offer. I said, *"There is only one problem with the barbecue."* *"What's that?"* he asked. Smiling, I announced, *"I am a vegetarian."* After a long silence, he said, *"We'll barbecue carrots then!"* We both laughed and I knew that I had waited long enough to make a friend.

While interruptions can be distracting, they don't need to derail you. Having a few ready responses will help you comfortably meet the situation.

Discuss, Learn, Apply

How do you respond when ...

1. ... little children disturb the Bible study?

2. ... the television is on?

3. ... neighbors, friends, or relatives show up during your Bible study?

4. ... you are offered food?

Chapter 18
Avoiding Common Mistakes

I feel I am qualified to speak on the subject of this chapter since much of what I've learned has come through the school of trial and error. The good thing about giving thousands of studies is there is always an opportunity to learn from the mistakes. In this chapter, I will share what I've discovered with the hope you will not need to repeat the same mistakes.

When I first began, I thought I needed to provide an ironclad case to prove every doctrine. In one of my early presentations on the Sabbath, I tortured my elderly students with a marathon study where we read over sixty separate Bible passages. By the appeal at the end, the poor victims were ready to agree to anything just to get me to leave their home.

Beginners commonly overload their studies with too much information. Counsel given to long-winded preachers also applies here. "Some of your lengthy discourses would have far better effect upon the people if cut up into three. The people cannot digest so much; their minds cannot even grasp it, and they become wearied and confused by having so much matter brought before them in one discourse. Two thirds of such long discourses are lost" (*Evangelism*, p. 176).

Another reason you want to keep your studies short and to the point is you want to become known as an interesting teacher. "If you stop when you should, giving them no more at once than they can comprehend and profit by, they will be eager to hear more, and thus the interest will be sustained. ... Let your discourses be short. ... that you may gain the reputation of being an interesting speaker" (*Evangelism*, p. 177).

Studying with four seminary students of another faith challenged me to keep our studies intensely interesting and stimulating. I knew I was succeeding when several weeks into the study one of the seminarians met me at the door and eagerly said, "*We have been waiting all week for you. Our study is all we can talk about.*"

While it is vital we allow the Bible to be the ultimate authority to establish our beliefs, it is unnecessary to proof text every statement we utter. There are many things people will accept at face value. Fifteen texts are usually more effective than thirty because people can absorb only a certain amount. If we overload them it causes conviction to diminish.

"It is not the best policy to be so very explicit, and say all upon a point that can be said, when a few arguments will cover the ground and be sufficient for all practical purposes to convince or silence opponents" (*Gospel Workers*, p. 376). "You need not feel that all the truth is to be spoken to unbelievers on any and every occasion. You should plan carefully what to say and what to leave unsaid" (*Evangelism*, p. 125).

Things to be left unsaid are statements that cannot be explicitly proven in the Bible even though they are revealed in the Spirit of Prophecy. There are teachings the Spirit of Prophecy brings out in clear relief that are only subtly insinuated in Scripture. While these are not critical doctrine, they are interesting. People who read the Spirit of Prophecy have a tendency to weave into their studies these unique insights with a certain air of authority. If you have a student who is well-versed in the Bible, they may find your insights intriguing and ask you to show where they can be found in the Scripture. Examples of this include: the Garden of Eden was taken to heaven before the flood; Mary Magdalene was the woman caught in adultery; and dinosaurs were not taken on the ark. While these things are inferred in the Bible, they should not be dogmatically presented. If you happen to mention such things, you can say the Bible seems to indicate this when several texts are compared.

Avoid dropping off study guides at the door like a pizza delivery person. You must become involved with people by spending time together. If your student doesn't allow you to enter their home, pray for ideas on how to get close to them. Take them a gift of a loaf of bread, something from your garden or another token. Perhaps this will break the ice. Through prayer, God will show you ways to remove barriers.

People who don't welcome your visit are usually not interested. If they also aren't completing their studies, they definitely are indifferent. Negligence may indicate a lack of interest, laziness or a learning disability. There are several things you can attempt to revive a student's interest if they are slow to complete their lessons, don't fill in the blanks in the study guides or miss their appointments. By addressing the situation in one of the following ways, you can discover the real problem and seek to resolve it. Try any of these approaches to jump-start your student: *"I've noticed you don't complete your lessons. Is there any way I can help?" "Are these studies interesting and helpful? If not, I have another set you may find more interesting." "I enjoy studying the Bible with you, but I don't want you to feel obligated. I've noticed you've not been making our appointments and I wonder if you still want to continue the lessons."*

If they don't put forth an honest effort to engage in the study, then you should present the gospel to them. If this doesn't convert them and lead them to be more active, then you should seriously consider not continuing your studies. For every student who is not genuinely interested in finding new truth and obeying God, there is another person who is receptive that is being neglected because you don't have time for them. Don't let the devil tie up your time with his decoys.

Avoid allowing your studies to become mere social visits. Some people, especially the elderly, enjoy your visit just for the company. Don't get sidetracked from your mission to study God's Word. Ask them if they are truly interested. *"Gertrude, I enjoy our friendship, but I've noticed you don't do the studies. Are you interested in them or is there something I can do to help you complete them? I like our visits together, but don't you think we both would be more blessed if we studied together? Is this okay with you?"*

It is important to be faithful in arriving on time for your appointments. If you set a pattern of canceling and rescheduling, the students will imitate you. Numerous times people have been surprised to see me show up at their house in some of the foulest weather. They've told me that when they felt like canceling a study they wouldn't because I had been so faithful in making our appointments. Our inconsistency and irregularity usually means the interest will not make a decision in favor of Christ and His truth.

As mentioned before, a very important skill to learn is how to avoid controversial subjects early on. "Do not at the outset press before the people the most objectionable features of our faith, lest you close their ears to those things which come as a new revelation" (*Evangelism*, p. 201). If you are asked about the Sabbath, speaking in tongues, secret rapture, tribulation, jewelry or diet early in your studies, say, *"That is a good question. Would you like to study this topic?"* (Wait for their answer.) *Let's study it as one of our lessons then, but I think it would fit better later in the series after we have covered some other things first. Would this be okay with you?"* Early in my experience, I lost more studies over this than what was necessary. Learn to defer these topics until the appropriate time.

Very inquisitive students have a way of constantly asking premature questions. If telling them you will answer their question in a future lesson becomes too repetitious, you can make a joke about it. I may smile broadly as I say, *"Now you know the answer to that question. Can you repeat it with me? 'We have a future study on that topic.'"* We both chuckle and the humor makes it easier for them to wait.

Remember to keep to the order of your lessons. Truth must be progressive. You don't want to get ahead of the studies. Allow the truth to come together piece by piece and to dawn on the conscience. "But the path of the just is as the shining light, that shineth more and more unto the perfect day" (Proverbs 4:18).

Don't do like one person I trained. He had a very interested family studying with him. For some unknown reason, this Bible instructor thought he would simplify the process and instead of handing his students the lessons one at a time each week, he decided to give all of the upcoming lessons to his students to keep in a notebook. He intended for them to study each lesson in order along with him. His students, though, possessed a normal curiosity to see what the future lessons were about. Naturally, they were attracted to read the mark of the beast lesson. They were so alarmed by what they read that they cancelled all future appointments and returned all of the materials to their Bible instructor. This man was so sorry for his indiscretion. He told me that the sad thing about it was that he was at the point where he was going to present the Sabbath. The lesson here is pretty obvious. Only give the studies you are ready to cover.

Along this same vein, do not give your student a full message book early on or they may be like the family I've just described. When at the outset students receive a book like *The Great Controversy*, you run a very high risk they will turn to the controversial chapters. These topics are much too interesting for people to restrain themselves from jumping to the back of the book. There definitely is a time to present full message books. Just wait until your student has accepted some of the foundational truths. Then use these books to reinforce your lessons.

Be careful not to spend too much time with a zealous believer of another faith whose goal is to convert you. They could be taking time God would have you spend with someone more receptive. Remember, "The perception and appreciation of truth ... depends less upon the mind than upon the heart. ... To those who ... having an honest desire to know and to do His will the truth is revealed as the power of God for their salvation" (*The Desire of Ages*, p. 455, 456). Conversion is your main goal and not convincing a person of doctrine. A converted person's attitude is "Teach me Thy way, O Lord; I will walk in thy truth" (Psalm 86:11). Spend time with people who have this position and help people who lack this adopt it.

While it is good to be enthusiastic, you want to avoid being overzealous. There is a way to be positive and not pushy. If you first win friendship, you will earn the right to persuade people to do the right thing.

Be careful not to stay too long in a home. While people may express keen interest, they will later come to the conclusion they can't afford the time. It is better to leave people wanting more than to saturate them. An hour is the longest you should be in a home.

Sometimes the person you think is your best prospect turns out not to obey the truth. And the person you didn't expect much from is the one who ends up being a true follower of Christ. This is why you want to give special attention to those who appear to be irreligious. Since they aren't connected to a church, they can be your best candidates. The unchurched also don't have erroneous doctrine to unlearn. They need to hear the basic gospel and be brought to Christ. Once they accept Him they are willing to learn and follow whatever the Bible teaches.

We haven't covered how to handle all the sticky situations you may find yourself in. I have a few more mistakes to make myself and I don't want to rob you of the adventure of making your own. Just remember no mistake is ever so large that God's marvelous blanket of grace can't cover it. Weep if you must. Apologize if you need to. But then smile and move on to the next study.

Discuss, Learn, Apply

1. Why is it better to keep the Bible study under an hour long and not give an overabundance of information in one study?

2. What can you do with people who are missing their study appointments or not completing their studies?

3. Explain why it is important to always be on time for your studies and why you should not cancel a study.

4. Is it a good policy to give to a Bible student a book that contains the full three-angels' message early in your studies? Explain.

Chapter 19
SPEND TIME WITH QUALIFIED PEOPLE

*I*t's a sad but true reality every Bible instructor must accept—not everyone is going to accept the truth. It is entirely possible to spend all your time with people who don't commit their lives to God. The devil likes for us to be consumed with such people.

If you are to be fruitful then it is imperative you learn how to discern who are the best candidates for studies. Jesus said, "Ye shall know them by their fruits. ... Every good tree bringeth forth good fruit" (Matthew 7:16–17). We are not to judge whether people will be saved or not, but we are to be fruit inspectors and determine which fruit is ripe for picking.

In the book *Gospel Workers*, Ellen White describes a dream she had that illustrates the need to find people who are ripe fruit for God. Ellen and some friends are picking berries in the dream. While she is intent to pick the ripe ones her friends complain that they can't find any suitable fruit. Mrs. White notices, "Some of the nice large berries had fallen to the ground, and were half consumed by worms and insects. 'O!' thought I, 'if this field had only been entered before, all this precious fruit might have been saved. But it is too late now'" (*Gospel Workers*, 1892 edition, p. 328, 329). Her friends made the mistake of overlooking the ripe fruit and caused it to be forever lost.

We should spend quality time with those who are ripe for the truth. Those who are green or nearly ripe should still get our attention but it should be proportionate to their interest level. If we spend the bulk of our time with the green fruit, we will find the ripe fruit will pass beyond the point of interest.

Some people are ripe to study last-day truths. Others are a little green, but nearly ripe. Then there are those who haven't even blossomed. How can we identify those who are ripe for Bible studies? Some characteristics of "ripe fruit" include people who:

✓ Manifest an earnest desire to seek and find Bible truth.

✓ Accept Bible studies and complete courses.

✓ Are lonely, unhappy and dissatisfied with their lives.

✓ Visit or attend your church regularly.

✓ Speak favorably of your church and its services.

✓ Accept major doctrines and make positive decisions.

✓ Display signs they are under conviction.

✓ Are dissatisfied with their own church.

✓ Don't belong to a church or are backsliders.

✓ Have evidenced a change in lifestyle as they've learned truth.

✓ Demonstrate a desire to share with others what they've learned.

✓ Are dependents who show signs of conversion and who will follow the positive decisions of their parents.

People who are green fruit typically refuse Bible studies or do not complete them, do not accept the clear teachings of Scripture no matter what has been tried, are deeply involved and strongly committed to their own church, continually talk despairingly about your church and its doctrines and are friendly but will not make a commitment. Just because someone might be classified as green fruit, it doesn't mean we shouldn't work for them. We should, however, allocate more of our time and energy for the ripe fruit people. Budgeting your time in this manner means more souls will be won.

Discuss, Learn, Apply

1. Why is it important to concentrate on people who are ripe and are making good progress?

2. How can you tell if someone is receptive to Bible truth?

3. How can you tell if someone is not receptive and is taking your time away from others?

Chapter 20
HOW TO GET FRIENDS TO CHURCH

*T*im attended a few nights of an evangelistic series in our city. His work kept him from coming to all the meetings, but I was able to schedule studies with him after the evangelist left town. Tim was an avid Bible student and we became good friends. When it came to keeping the Sabbath, however, he dragged his feet. Every week he had some other commitment to keep him from God's house. Most often, it was racing cars at the track. I knew Tim believed the Sabbath was on Saturday and that we should keep it. His problem was he did not place it as a high priority.

After one study I asked, *"Tim, what is your ultimate goal in life?"* He thought for a moment and then sincerely replied, *"It is to live fully for God and to allow His purpose to be realized in my life."* I affirmed his answer and then challenged him. *"Tim, if this is your goal, how do you plan to fulfill it when you are disobeying a Bible command you know to be true?"* Tim quizzically looked at me and asked what I was talking about. *"You are breaking the Sabbath every week you go to the race track and not to church,"* I said, while trying not to sound confrontational. I continued, *"I know you love God and want to follow Him, but how are you going to achieve your full potential if you continue to neglect to obey what the Lord has shown you?"*

I could tell from the look in his eyes my simple appeal had reached his heart. *"You're right,"* he confessed, *"I will be in church next Sabbath."* Not long after, Tim officially joined our church. My approach was rather direct, but I could venture to be blunt because I had earned this right as his friend. This is all part of winning confidence and having people trust you as someone who has their best interest at heart.

Many people may take studies, but how do you encourage them to attend church or an evangelistic series? Though there is no completely foolproof method, there are some principles that can help you succeed.

A lot depends upon the quality of the interest. If a person is a casual seeker, it is more difficult for them to walk in the light. Someone hot on the trail of truth, on the other hand, cannot be held back. No matter the degree of commitment, all are to be encouraged to follow God.

It is vital to call for decisions to follow Christ at the close of all your studies. Don't wait until the end of the series. Learn to ask for decisions early. Accepting Jesus as Saviour means we accept His death and sinless life in our behalf to save us from sin's wages. We are also called to honor Him as Lord. This requires that we allow Him to be the Master and Ruler of every facet of our life. We are not our own. We have been purchased with God's blood. If we accept Him as Lord, we will obediently follow His leading.

This next point is very useful to get people to attend evangelistic meetings. God has blessed my work by bringing the majority of my students to seminars to make decisions. The way I encourage them to attend is the secret to this success. If I am preparing for a seminar, I like to start a large number of studies nine to twelve weeks before opening night. Either you alone or a team can do this. Set a goal of at least thirty studies or much more if your church can do it.

In the pre-meeting studies, I seek to accomplish three objectives. First, I want to develop a friendship and win confidence. It's easy to invite friends to attend. They know we are not trying to trick them into anything and that if they become uncomfortable with the meetings we will still be their friend. The second goal is to lead the student to Christ. If we can teach them how to trust and obey Jesus, they will more likely accept the truth taught in the seminar.

The third objective is to lay a foundation for the testing truths they will encounter. The order of topics is very important in accomplishing this. You want to completely avoid testing truth before the meeting. Your goal is not to convince the students of the truth so much as it is to get them to the meeting. By covering in your pre-meeting lessons all the foundational subjects necessary for understanding the Sabbath, but without getting into it, we prepare them to accept this new truth. By the time your student hears the evangelist present the Sabbath during the second week of the series, they will have had the groundwork prepared twice--once by you and another by the evangelist. This makes them especially prepared.

Through the years I've seen people give scores of studies, but few Bible instructors succeed at getting their students to attend meetings. Here are two crucial things that will encourage them to transfer from you to the evangelist.

First, make your student aware of the upcoming seminar. Have a goal to do this at least by the second study if not before. Always describe the lessons as "introductory to the public seminar." (Never say "evangelistic meeting" or call the speaker an "evangelist." He is a "seminar speaker" and the series is a "public Bible seminar." Evangelism has negative connotations for most.) I will often do this either during the time I canvass them or by the second study. Here is an example of how to introduce the public seminar when offering studies. This is best done later in your presentation after they have made an appointment to study with you:

"Mrs. Jones, these studies are introductory lessons to Bible prophecy and are offered for a limited time. I know you will get a lot out of them. Let me tell you about a seminar that is also coming to town. In a few weeks, a Christian ministry that holds adult Bible education meetings is going to conduct a prophecy seminar right here in our town. I have volunteered to share these introductory lessons with people in preparation for this event. People from all the different churches and even non-church people will attend. My students who take these introductory lessons will find they really learn the Bible better than they ever have before. You'll be interested to know this method of study has been successfully used around the world and it is being offered for the first time here in this city by volunteers like me."

Of course, you can word this anyway that suits you. Just be upbeat about the benefits of the "introductory lessons" and the "public seminar." A reason to do this in the canvass is the people who commit to study are most likely also interested in attending the seminar. This results in a higher percentage of transfers.

If you're concerned that mentioning the seminar in the initial canvass may jeopardize scheduling a study with a good interest, wait until the first or second study when you have established rapport. In this case you will say, *"By the way, John, did I tell you about the Bible seminar coming to town?* (They will answer that you haven't.) *It's going to be a community Bible seminar that people from all religious persuasions will attend. The studies you and I are doing are introductory lessons and are designed to provide a background in Bible prophecy* (or "in the Bible" if you are not covering prophecy) *so they will get more out of the public seminar. I am a volunteer and am only able to do this for a limited time. The public classes will go into more depth and detail as the speaker covers the prophecies relevant for our time. If you like these studies you will probably enjoy the seminar."*

Notice that the first time you mention this, it is done as a soft sell. You have nothing to urge. Say it in a relaxed, casual manner and include phrases like *"you will probably enjoy the seminar."* In future studies, after confidence has developed, become more positive and state *"you are really going to enjoy this seminar,"* or *"you've done so well with these lessons, I know you will find the public seminar to be a blessing."* Constantly find opportunity to frequently mention the seminar during the nine weeks or more leading up to the meeting.

Four weeks before the series encourage them to put the dates for the first five nights on their calendar. (Avoid telling them it goes for several weeks. If they feel it is too long they might lose interest.) When they ask where it is going to be held, you can tell them you will get the information for them, but you *do* know it begins on this or that date. If you are using pre-registration for seats (which is always recommended), ask if they'd like a ticket. Bring it the next week and pre-register them for reserved seating and materials.

Three weeks before the meetings, say, *"I am looking forward to attending the public seminar, but I don't want to go by myself. What do you think about us going and sitting together?"* Two weeks before, bring a copy of the advertising flyer to your student. Let them know this is the seminar you've been telling them about. Be enthusiastic and positive about their attendance. Emphasize again you want to sit together. If they need a ride, make arrangements for them to go with you. Encourage their spouse and other family members to attend and reserve seats for them.

Continue to reference the meetings as a community seminar. Make sure a handbill is mailed to their home. And double check to see if their area will receive the general mailing of handbills by the post office. The week of the meetings, bring another handbill to them. Ask them if they received the general handbill mailing. Again, make arrangements to sit together.

Always build the seminar speaker's reputation. Assure them they will enjoy his teaching style. If it is not being too pushy, call your student the day before and day of the meetings to again arrange a ride if needed and to make sure you reserved enough seats. During this last call, you can agree where you will meet at the seminar hall.

The second part of the equation to transfer your students is not to be missed. You've undoubtedly heard the old saying, *"You can lead a horse to water, but you can't make him drink."* But have you ever heard the optimists' version? He adds, *"You can't make him drink, but you can salt his oats."* You can give Bible studies and *encourage* people to attend a seminar, but you can't *make* them attend. You can, however, make them thirsty for the meetings. With a little skill, you can pique their curiosity and create an insatiable desire to attend.

How do you salt the oats? It's easy. In almost every study find a way to reference the seminar as a source for more information than you are able to provide. When studying Daniel 2's climactic end with the second coming you can salt the oats by saying, *"Margie, you've heard about the rapture haven't you? This is what the Bible is describing here when the Rock smites the image's feet. We don't have time to cover it in our study, but do you remember the seminar I told you about? The speaker is going to teach what the Bible really says about the rapture. A lot of people have questions about whether it will be pre-tribulation or post-tribulation. The seminar speaker will reveal exactly what the Bible says. You don't want to miss it."*

In a study on Daniel 3, you will compare the experience of the three Hebrews with that of people in the last days as described in Revelation 13. You get your salt shaker out and sprinkle into your study, *"We don't have time in these introductory lessons to study who the antichrist beast is or what his mark is, but the speaker for the seminar will have several presentations on these topics. He will take all the Bible says on the beast and chart it on a big screen along with pictures of the beasts from Daniel and Revelation. You will love it when you see how he makes this very plain."*

Something in every study lends itself to salting the oats. In fact, my *Prophecies of Hope* lessons include a special "salting the oats" feature in each lesson. The "Looking Forward" section helps create a desire for the future lessons. This motivates students to continue the studies and it can also be used to get them interested in the upcoming evangelistic series.

The more you build what the evangelist is going to teach the more you heighten their anticipation. Soon they will catch your enthusiasm and will not want to miss a single night. Make your student's thirst for the meetings as strong as that of a man's lost in the desert for a gushing spring of fresh water. If you succeed in doing this, nothing will keep them from the meetings.

Much of my Bible study work has been done in connection with seminars. I have found these methods to be very effective in getting people to attend and you will, too, as you prayerfully apply them. If you are not working towards a seminar, it will be your responsibility to teach the testing truths and to encourage your student to obey God. Getting them to church is the first hurtle towards baptism. After your student has learned the Sabbath, wait a couple of weeks for it to settle in and develop conviction. Then invite them to church.

You will have the best success if you invite them to a special service. Remember this invitation is not for membership or even to make a life-long commitment to keep the Sabbath holy. It is just an opportunity for them to come and see what church is like.

Special programs your student will delight to attend are musical concerts, guest speakers or a special Bible study that is non-member friendly. Be careful with all of these options. You need to make sure the people doing the program are safe for non-members. Sometimes our people have lived so long in their Christian cocoon, they don't know how they sound to others. There are too many unfortunate experiences where guests are turned off by someone not being sensitive to the fact that non-believers are present.

One Sabbath my wife brought four of her co-workers to church for the first time. Sherilyn was scheduled to play her flute for special music and she invited a colleague to do a flute duet with her. They practiced for several weeks at the hospital where they worked. Several of the nurses decided to attend to see them play. It was very unfortunate, but the pastor decided to have a mixed salad sermon that day. He tossed into it every thing that distinguishes our church as unique. We heard a little about vegetarianism, some warnings against dancing and movies, laments over jewelry, critiques against people who seek to enforce Sunday worship and the mark of the beast, and very little that was appropriate for a first time attendee. Sherilyn and I felt like crawling under the pew. Our guests left church wondering how such a nice person like my wife could belong to such a kooky church.

I am convinced more of our people don't invite their friends and family to church because of similar situations. A lady told me she brought her sister to her church for the first time. They arrived a little early for Sabbath School and as they were waiting for the teacher to get there, one of the dear saints decided he would make a point. Looking over at the non-member sister who was wearing jewelry, he suggested, *"While we are waiting for the teacher, why don't we discuss why good Christians don't wear jewelry."* This lady was mortified and vowed never to invite another person. This man was just what the devil ordered that morning.

I once announced to my members a unique church service that would be entirely sensitive to our guests. No one would say or do anything that could embarrass them if they chose to bring a guest to church on the appointed Sabbath. The announcements would be positive and not scolding. The special music would be performed by people who could truly inspire. And the sermon would be evangelistic. When the promised day arrived, our attendance soared sixty-two percent. I even met a guest who was invited by a not-so-committed member. When I asked him where Melody was, he told me, *"O, she's not able to come because she had to work today. But I wouldn't miss it for anything."* Even our most marginal members want to be proud of their church. We found it absolutely amazing when five people enrolled in Bible studies that day and were eventually baptized. Our church was on fire! (I wish every church would assign at least one Sabbath a quarter as a "safe Sabbath" for inviting guests. I believe we would see a large influx of people. Why don't you give it a try and let me know how it goes.)

Before you invite your friend to church, you should call your pastor and let him know your plan. Inquire if there is a Sabbath more suitable than another for them to come. Don't be shy to ask what his sermon is about. You only have one opportunity to make a first impression. Don't leave it to chance. He most likely wants to keep his foot out of his mouth as much as you do. Both of you surely don't want your friends' introduction to be a controversial sermon that is premature for them. Don't be like the family who invited their Catholic friends to church on religious liberty Sabbath. The sermon was a warning against the stealthy advance of the pope into the political arena. It was truthful enough—just very poor timing for a Catholic's first exposure to us. Afterwards, the pastor felt terrible that he didn't know these dear people were present.

One very effective way to invite your student to church is for you to arrange to sing special music, preach or teach a Sabbath School class. It goes without saying that you must have the gift to do these things. If you sing as poorly as I do and attempt to do special music, you're sure to discourage them from returning. In my case, my students would be embarrassed to sit with me through the rest of the service. Assuming you are gifted in whatever you choose, they will delight in giving you moral support. You can tell them, *"It would really mean a lot to me to have you there. Can you come?"* This is also effective if you have children who are going to participate in the service and your students know your children.

Don't overload your guests on their first Sabbath. For some people a full day of sabbath school, church service and dinner afterwards may be more "religion" than they can handle. Let the Spirit lead, but it is better to leave a person wanting more than for them to get spiritual indigestion.

For an ongoing program to attract non-members, you can start a special Bible study class during Sabbath School. Offer it for a limited time of six to eight weeks. Cover topics that especially interest new people. Bible prophecy is always a good option. After several weeks, gradually entice the interests to stay for church by having a special service to invite them to. Once you cycle through the short course, you can offer another one again when you have more non-members ready to invite

It isn't difficult to get your students to church. By combining the principles of winsome witnessing and the ideas in this chapter, you will feel the joy of seeing your friends walk through the doors of your sanctuary.

Discuss, Learn, Apply

1. How many studies should a church seek to give in preparation for an evangelistic series?

2. What are three objectives you want to accomplish during your pre-evangelistic meeting Bible studies?

3. What are two things you must do if you want your Bible students to transfer from the home study to an evangelistic meeting?

4. List how to make multiple invitations to the meetings over a four week period leading up to an evangelistic meeting.

5. Give examples of "salting the oats" for different types of studies.

6. What are some ways you can successfully invite a Bible student to church?

Chapter 21
OVERCOMING OBSTACLES TO DECISIONS

*E*lla and James faithfully attended each night of my evangelistic meeting. They eagerly accepted every doctrine and indicated their desire to be baptized and join our church. But all of this suddenly changed at the end of the series during a Sabbath School class where Ella learned what God's Word says about jewelry. She was so furious I thought I saw blistering hot steam whistling out of her ears.

Ella skipped the meeting later that evening and stayed awake until the sun came up the next morning studying every Bible text on adornment. I made an appointment with James to visit them early Sunday. When I arrived at their home, I found Ella was still fuming. She met me grim faced and armed with her notebook of handwritten notes made during her midnight research.

We reviewed several of her questions until I was impressed to change the subject. I gently suggested, *"Ella, let's put our discussion on jewelry aside for a moment. Is there anything else you've learned that you have questions about or don't agree with?"* When she told me she agreed with everything except this one subject, I offered, *"Ella, you have told me you want to be baptized and become a part of God's remnant church. Let's review the major teachings of the Bible that our church emphasizes and prepare you for baptism."*

I began asking Ella and James the doctrinal review questions, knowing the first five dealt with conversion. They were to answer affirmatively after each question if they agreed with that point of belief. When I read the statement, *"I have surrendered every area of my life to Jesus to walk in all His ways known to me or to be made known,"* James confidently replied he had, but Ella sat silently. Casting her gaze down, she slowly shook her head and finally whispered, *"No."*

I thanked Ella for being so honest and then asked if she would like to surrender her life and feel the peace of God. Thankfully, she said she would welcome this experience. For the next several minutes I carefully explained the gospel and then we all knelt in prayer. It was a very emotional moment with the Holy Spirit present. There wasn't a dry eye in our circle. After the prayer, Ella rose from her knees as her hands grappled with the tiny earrings in her ears. Unable to remove them, she turned to James and said, *"Please, help me get these things out. I don't want them anymore."*

Be sure to bring people to Christ before introducing testing truths. Once they have accepted Jesus, they will be more prepared to obey Him. "In order to break down the barriers of prejudice and impenitence the love of Christ must have a part in every discourse. Make men to know how much Jesus loves them, and what evidences He has given them of His love. What love can equal that which God has manifested for man by the death of Christ on the cross. When the heart is filled with the love of Jesus, this can be presented to the people and it will affect hearts" (*Evangelism*, p. 285).

Some would propose, *"Why the big concern over adornment? It is such a small thing."* On the surface it appeared Ella's problem was with jewelry. But this was only a symptom. Her inner heart issue of conversion was much more significant. If I had glossed over this teaching Ella would have missed the opportunity to surrender self and find Jesus as the King of Peace.

We must recognize conversion comes with a test. The word "conversion" literally means to completely turn around and make a full surrender. If we smooth the path to God by removing all the tests, we only assist people to assume a form of religion without experiencing the real transforming power of the Spirit.

This can be especially true with the dress question. "The idolatry of dress is a moral disease. It must not be taken over into the new life. In most cases, submission to the gospel requirements will demand a decided change in the dress" (*Testimonies for the Church*, Vol. 6, p. 96).

It is important to teach what the Bible reveals on dress, diet and other lifestyle-related issues, but this must always be done with the focus on Christ. "They say, 'You don't dress as you should.' They try to pick off the ornaments, or whatever seems offensive, but they do not seek to fasten the mind to the truth. Those who seek to correct others should present the attractions of Jesus. They should talk of His love and compassion, present His example and sacrifice, reveal His Spirit, and they need not touch the subject of dress at all. There is no need to make the dress question the main point of your religion. There is something richer to speak of. Talk of Christ, and when the heart is converted, everything that is out of harmony with the Word of God will drop off. It is only labor in vain to pick leaves off a living tree. The leaves will reappear. The ax must be laid at the root of the tree, and then the leaves will fall off, never to return" (*Evangelism*, p. 272).

When Ella gave her heart to Jesus the adornment couldn't come off fast enough. This is the reason we need to appeal frequently with the

Cross. "Christ crucified—talk it, pray it, sing it, and it will break and win hearts" (*Testimonies for the Church*, Vol. 6, p. 67).

Ella and James never regretted their decision to follow Jesus and join his church. They didn't consider the measly price they paid too expensive when they looked at Calvary. For several years they basked in the love of their new church family. Early one morning as they were sleeping in bed, Ella and James were brutally murdered when their wayward grandson heartlessly shot them. They rest now awaiting the Life Giver's call at the second coming. Their selfless and Spirit-filled life assures me they will feel Jesus' embrace on resurrection morning. I am so glad God led me to allow His tests to try the heart and lead this precious couple into eternal life.

When assisting people to make positive decisions for truth, you need to speak to their heart more than their intellect. They must feel you genuinely are there to help them make a choice that is in their best interest. "Each one should be asked how he is going to take these things, if he is going to make a personal application of them. And then you should watch and see if there is an interest in this one or that. Five words spoken to them privately will do more than the whole discourse has done" (*Evangelism*, p. 285).

Don't ask people to keep the Sabbath only because it is the right day. Invite them instead to follow Jesus and show their love for Him by keeping His Sabbath holy (John 14:15). Don't tell people to join your church. Rather encourage them to heed the voice of the Shepherd to be gathered into His one fold He is calling people into (John 10:16). Make every appeal focus on Jesus. Talk often of how He died for their sins and is leading them by His Spirit and Word (John 16:13; 17:17).

Have clearly in mind the decision you will ask for at the end of each lesson. "As you present testing truth, ask often, who is now willing, as they have heard the words of God, pointing out their duty, to consecrate their hearts and minds, with all their affections, to Christ Jesus" (*Evangelism*, p. 284) Sometimes all it takes is to read the decision question on the lesson guide. Point out the happiness and benefits that come from deciding to obey God. Have your student express their decision in their own words, because expression deepens impression.

Ask action-oriented questions in all your studies. Once people agree to minor action, they are more likely to agree to a major action. *"Richard, how does what we learned today affect your life? How is God asking you to apply this truth?"* The journey to baptism and discipleship is made one step at a time, so make your appeals progressive in their application.

At the end of each study you need to ascertain if they understand the topic well enough to decide. To accomplish this, you will ask diagnostic questions that provide a chance to express objections. You don't want objections stacking up from one study to the next. If this happens, you will find it impossible to bring a person to a decision. Help them get their questions answered and perplexities erased as they arise.

"Many a laborer fails in his work because he does not come close to those who most need his help. With the Bible in hand, he should seek in a courteous manner to learn the objections which exist in the minds of those who are beginning to inquire, 'What is truth?' Carefully and tenderly should he lead and educate them, as pupils in a school. Many have to unlearn theories which they have long believed to be truth. As they become convinced that they have been in error concerning Bible subjects, they are thrown into perplexity and doubt. They need the tenderest sympathy and the most judicious help; they should be carefully instructed, and should be prayed for and prayed with, watched and guarded with the kindest solicitude" (*Gospel Workers*, p. 190, 191).

On the major testing truths you should ask the following questions in this order: "*What do you think about what we read from the Bible in this study?*" "*Do any questions on this topic come to your mind?*" "*Have you always understood what the Bible teaches (about the second coming; death is a sleep; etc.)?*"

This should surface any objections a person might have. If some *do* come to light, you will need to patiently help them find satisfying answers. Once they indicate they clearly understand, you need to move to an action question. You can say, "*Would you like to kneel together and tell God you are thankful ... (He is coming soon; death is a peaceful sleep and He is the Life Giver; the Sabbath is on Saturday, etc.)?*"

You don't want to move too quickly for a decision on the Sabbath. I generally wait until the second Sabbath study before I ask for this decision. This is such a revolutionary subject to most people that you need to give them a little space to process it.

Years ago, I discovered the importance of this while serving as evangelism coordinator for a dozen evangelists. One day, our guys remarked that they were losing a lot of people when they presented the Sabbath topic and then immediately following it with how the Sabbath was changed and with the Sunday texts. (Some even preached on the mark of the beast soon after these presentations.) Putting too many Sabbath messages together without giving adequate time for people to process what they are hearing is like a boxer using the combination one, two, three knockout punch. People were falling out on all sides. Our evangelists decided to change. After presenting the first Sabbath message, they now move to a more neutral subject. Several nights later they may return to the Sabbath and later to the mark of the beast.

Do something similar when giving personal studies. The intensity of an evangelistic meeting isn't present in home studies, but speaking on the Sabbath three or four weeks in a row could be too much for your student. After the second presentation be sure to ask diagnostic questions. I like to phrase them in this order:*" Susan, have you ever studied the Sabbath before or is this new to you?" "Do you have any questions on the Sabbath or is it clear to you that it is on our seventh-day of the week?" "What do you think about keeping the Sabbath?"* (This may be followed by, *"Does your job require you to work on Saturday?"*)

If they say they look forward to keeping the Sabbath, you can end your visit with prayer. If the answer is they are not sure about keeping it, you can ask them the reason. You may have other objections to answer or you may simply need to listen to their concerns and then end with, *"Susan, I know you love Jesus and if He were personally here to ask you to keep His Sabbath holy you would tell him you want to keep it because you love him, don't you? Let's kneel and pray together and ask Him to show you from the Bible what He wants you to do. I know this is new to you, but if this is what the Bible teaches, I know you will want to do it. So let's pray and tell Jesus this, okay?"*

Depending on how you presented the Sabbath, some people will agree it is on Saturday but not feel a need to keep it. This usually happens when the Sabbath is presented before the antichrist subject. Without the context of the war between Christ and Satan, most people view it only as a matter of choosing a day in seven. If this is your situation, you will need to wait until they have studied the beast and how the Sabbath was changed or even until the mark of the beast before urging a decision.

Most people process a Sabbath decision in three phases. Understanding this will help you keep your appeals synchronized with where they are. When they first learn of the Sabbath, people will say, *"That's interesting. I can see we need to keep one day as the Sabbath."* Or they may remark, *"I don't really do anything on Saturday anyway."* At this point they have not made the connection they should be going to church on the Sabbath. You will find it useful to hold back on urging church attendance at this stage.

The second stage usually follows a study on the change of the Sabbath, beast, or mark of the beast and is more of a question. *"Can I go to my church on Sunday and then keep the Sabbath at home?"* Others will even suggest, *"Can I go to my church on Sunday and then to yours on Saturday?"* You want to encourage church attendance on Sabbath and assure them the Lord will help them understand what they should do otherwise. It is best to refrain from advising a complete separation from their church at this point. This is left for the next stage.

The third stage takes place after they have studied the remnant church and how to come out of Babylon. Now your student should totally understand the decision they need to make. This is the time to encourage them to fully follow Jesus and keep His Sabbath holy by becoming a part of His remnant church. If they are not ready to be baptized, you certainly want to advocate they begin attending church.

There are four categories of people as it relates to decision-making. There are those who are willing to make a decision and are able to follow through with it. Their employment doesn't conflict with keeping the Sabbath holy. Neither is their family threatening them if they obey the Lord. These people can easily make a decision.

More difficult are those who are willing to decide in favor of truth, but work or family make them feel they're unable to change. Ask diagnostic questions to find out what is holding them back: *"Is anything preventing you from keeping God's Sabbath holy?" "How will your employer feel about you taking Sabbath's off and going to church?" "How does your family feel about the changes in your life and your decision to follow Christ and become a part of His remnant people?"*

Once you discover obstacles, help them think through options that permit them to be loyal to God. Pray with them and for them. More importantly, teach them how to pray for themselves. Lead them to claim God's promises. Sympathize if they have a predicament, but then say, *"This is a problem, but God has the solution. I have been praying about this and God has impressed me to read this text. I believe He gave me this for you."* Have the person read a promise to inspire their faith.

A decision comes when the student exercises faith to be obedient. Encourage them with the thought that as they exercise their faith, faith will increase. Lead them to make a full surrender of their life. "As souls give themselves to the Lord Jesus, making an entire surrender, they will understand the doctrine" (*Evangelism*, p. 465).

For those encountering Sabbath work problems, I like to tell the story of how God led His people out of Egypt. When the Israelites approach the Red Sea, they are trapped with the water before them, mountains on both sides and Pharaoh's army fast approaching from behind. It looks like there is no way to escape. Then God performs a miracle. He makes a dry path through the sea and they are able to cross without getting their feet wet.

Forty years later, the scene is slightly different. Israel stands before the Jordan River at flood stage. It is perhaps two miles across. God commands them to cross into Canaan. This time God does not part the water. They have to move forward by faith. The priests bearing the ark wade into the murky water and when it reaches their ankles God dries up a path across the river.

These two ways God used to lead His people into the Promised Land illustrate how He leads us today. When God calls us to move forward, sometimes He makes it easy. Like He did at the Red Sea, He opens a plain path. We get the Sabbath off as soon as we ask for it. But at other times our faith is tested and we have to step into the water. In either case, God provides a way for us to obey Him.

Then I appeal, *"Mary, I don't know what your experience will be. When you ask your employer for Sabbaths off, you may find God gives you a Red Sea experience and you get it off without a problem. Or you might find you have to wade into a Jordan River experience. I don't know which it will be. But I do know this: God is faithful and He will open the way. He might allow your faith to be tested, but I promise He will deliver you. Will you trust Him? Will you give Him an opportunity to give you a Red Sea experience? And will you trust Him if it is a Jordan?"* This powerful appeal has helped many step out in faith for God.

Words brimming with faith inspire others with courage to obey. When your student faces obstacles, echo Caleb, "Let us go up at once, and possess it; for we are well able to overcome it" (Numbers 13:30). Memorize the following promise and share it often. "Our heavenly Father has a thousand ways to provide for us of which we know nothing. Those who accept the one principle of making the service of God supreme will find perplexities vanish and a plain path before their feet" (*The Ministry of Healing*, p. 481).

Relating stories of how God has provided for those in similar circumstance is very helpful. One gentleman I know was a barber when he first learned of the Sabbath. Saturdays were his busiest day. When he gave his heart to the Lord he knew he had to trust God and obey His Word. So Phil closed his barbershop on Saturdays and opened it on Sundays. Against all odds, his business increased.

Another friend was struggling with the Sabbath. Her employer told her there was no way he could let her have it off. It was clear she would need to find another job. Denise went job hunting while she continued to work. Her search for suitable employment continued to fail. Then she was challenged with the thought, *"You are not willing to quit breaking God's law until you find another job. You are depending too much on yourself. Perhaps the Lord wants you to trust Him."* Denise was so convicted she gave her notice on Friday and did not work another Sabbath. The following Monday she went job searching again and within hours found one that paid more money, had better hours, and was within walking distance of her house.

Finding another job that allows you to honor the Lord's Day is not always easy. One man had to leave a very lucrative career with a Fortune 500 company so that he could keep the Sabbath. Wherever he went to interview, he found his path blocked by his irate former boss. For a year his family struggled to make ends meet. The lifestyle supported by his executive salary was completely gone. *"Did he make the right decision?"* they wondered. The man decided to fill the empty hours of his day by resuming a long neglected hobby of painting landscapes. His busy career had kept him from the brushes for many years. He soon discovered he had not lost the artist's touch and it wasn't long before people heard about his work. This man found he was able to make a very comfortable living doing what he loved most—painting. What if he had compromised God's Word? He would have never discovered his potential as a commercial artist. God's way is always best even when we go through trying times.

By telling faith-building stories, your student will be inspired with courage. You can use my stories or your own. *Amazing Facts* publishes an excellent book of stirring Sabbath victory testimonies. The book is *Trials and Triumph* by Crystal Earnhardt.

Appeal to those in the valley of decision to allow God to be the Almighty in their life. He mercifully permits dark trials to teach us not to depend upon ourselves, but to trust Him in full obedience. What better time to lean upon Him than when we are seeking to follow His Word? He delights to prove Himself strong in our behalf. *"Let's give God the opportunity to be the Provider of our needs so we can watch Him work as we move forward by faith,"* is my appeal.

There are times when the reason a person is hesitating is not apparent. Prayer is very useful in sleuthing out the true source. God will give you insights you can't get any other way. I was visiting with a family that had been attending my meetings. They were all members except the husband. Despite being a truck driver who often had to be on the road, he arranged his schedule to attend the meetings. Dave agreed with everything taught, but a nasty tobacco habit stood in the way of his baptism. When I visited his home it dawned on me tobacco wasn't his problem at all. The real issue was his wife's family. They dominated their little country church. His father-in-law was an elder, his wife's brothers and sisters and their families were all members. Dave was the only non-member in the clan. The extended family was so interested in his conversion that they hounded him for years to make a decision. And all this time Dave hid behind his tobacco habit. He knew they would not permit him to be baptized as long as he used the poisonous weed. The Lord enlightened my mind during our visit that Dave could overcome tobacco anytime he desired. His hidden concern was he wanted his baptismal decision to truly be his choice and he didn't want it to appear he had given into his wife.

Outside his house, I pulled Dave aside from the family for a private conversation. I said, *"I believe you can overcome tobacco anytime you desire. The real issue here is you don't want it to appear your wife has won the religion debate after all these years. You want this to be your decision don't you?"* He sheepishly smiled as if I were the first person to catch on to his game. Then I suggested, *"What if we make this your decision? You believe this truth, don't you?"* He answered he did. *"Then let's not tell your wife you are going to be baptized. You can appear in the baptistery on Sabbath morning and surprise her and all the rest of the family. Then they will know it was your decision and you will have the pleasure of shocking and pleasing them at the same time. What do you think?"* Dave agreed to this plan and quit using tobacco that very moment.

Our agreement to keep this a secret would have worked except for one thing. The transformation in Dave's heart was so evident that it was written all over his face. When he went inside the house his wife and children kindly badgered him to reveal our secret. His wife eagerly interrogated, *"You're going to be baptized aren't you? Yes. I can see it in your eyes. You have a peace you didn't have before."* It wasn't long before Dave confessed and thrilled his loving wife. Soon phones were ringing from one end of the continent to the other. Friends and family from far away called to congratulate Dave. On Sabbath morning, when he went into the baptistery free from tobacco and pride, Dave had the peace of heaven in his heart. The obstacles to his peace were now completely removed.

Discuss, Learn, Apply

1. What was Ella's root issue?

2. When someone makes a decision for Christ, there will be tests. Why should we not remove these tests?

3. Why is asking for a decision after every Bible study so important?

4. Describe the three phases people typically go through to process a Sabbath decision.

5. How can you help a person make a positive decision for Jesus and His truth when they are facing obstacles?

6. What are some ways you can encourage a person to make a Sabbath decision when they are fearful?

Chapter 22
DECISION SIGNALS

I was visiting a lady who appeared to be turning away from the truth she had learned in my seminar. During our visit, Victoria revealed her fear that her husband would make good on his threat to leave her if she was baptized. After expressing my sympathy, we read Matthew 10:34-39 together.

"Think not that I am come to send peace on earth: I came not to send peace, but a sword. For I am come to set a man at variance against his father, and the daughter against her mother, and the daughter in law against her mother in law. And a man's foes shall be they of his own household. He that loveth father or mother more than me is not worthy of me: and he that loveth son or daughter more than me is not worthy of me. And he that taketh not his cross, and followeth after me, is not worthy of me. He that findeth his life shall lose it: and he that loseth his life for my sake shall find it."

Lifting my Bible before Victoria, I said with deep sincerity in my voice, *"We don't know what your husband will really do. If your marriage has been strained, Jesus is the only answer. I can promise you this, based on the Word of God I hold in my hands, if you trust God and follow what you know to be right, God will take care of you. I promise if you are faithful you will look back one year from now and say, 'God has been faithful.' I can't make this decision for you, but you can. You can trust God and obey Him. Victoria, you can feel the joy one year from now of knowing He has been very good to you because of your faith. Will you do it? Will you trust Jesus?"*

In the face of her husband's threats, Victoria was baptized. A year later, I happened to be preaching in that church. Victoria was there and she shared her testimony with the congregation. As tears streamed down her cheeks and her voice choked with emotion, she related the events of the night of our visit. Then she told how the year had proven my promise true. Her husband had a change of heart and was now attending with her.

There is a golden moment when people are ready to act. This is when you must ask for a decision. I knew this moment had arrived for Victoria when she told me she couldn't be baptized because of her husband. She already had made the decision to follow Jesus in her heart. My role was to help her find faith and release from her fear. What are other signals people give that they are ready to submit to Christ? Spot these and then persuade them to follow the Lord:

- ✓ *"I wish my husband were more agreeable to my becoming an Adventist."*
- ✓ *"I wonder if I would lose my job if I asked for the Sabbath off?"*
- ✓ *"I have some tithe to give you."*
- ✓ *"Would I have to quit ... (smoking, wearing jewelry, etc.)?"*
- ✓ *"What would I do all day Saturday?"*
- ✓ *"What will my friends think of me?"*
- ✓ *"How can I be sure the Lord will accept me?"*
- ✓ *"How many Bible studies must I take before I am ready?"*
- ✓ *"How long does it take to prepare for baptism?"*
- ✓ *"I am not sure my faith is strong enough."*

Our emotions influence the decisions we make. I've seen even the most logical men give into a temptation to buy a sporty pickup truck or flashy boat because of the good feelings they envision their new toy will bring. Our Creator made us to feel emotion. He does not ignore it and neither should we. We should present the beauties of Christ with a compelling smile, weep over the cost of the cross, and rejoice in the hope of heaven. Heartfelt appeals that focus on benefits to the obedient are powerful to encourage people to choose Christ. God will honor decisions based on solid biblical truth and married to a heart melted by the love of God.

"We must have more than an intellectual belief in the truth. Many of the Jews were convinced that Jesus was the Son of God, but they were too proud and ambitious to surrender. They decided to resist the truth, and they maintained their opposition. They did not receive into the heart the truth as it is in Jesus. When truth is held as truth only by the conscience, when the heart is not stimulated and made receptive, only the mind is affected. But when the truth is received as truth by the heart, it has passed through the conscience, and has captivated the soul with its pure principles. It is placed in the heart by the Holy Spirit, who reveals its beauty to the mind, that its transforming power may be seen in the character" (*Review and Herald*, Feb. 14, 1899).

Doctrinal texts are fine for convincing the mind. We need to combine these with other Scriptures that will appeal to the heart and tip the scales in the right direction. Victoria initially was convinced of the doctrine, but she still was unable to decide in favor of it. However, when we read from Matthew 10 the Word transformed her. Every soul-winner should have a reservoir of texts to share when hearts are looking for direction. Below are a few you can write in the flyleaf of your Bible to have ready.

Ultimately, you want to help your student set a date for baptism. *"Elizabeth, you have learned some precious Bible truths. God has blessed you, hasn't He? How would you like to set a date for your baptism? How does early or late October sound?"* If they have one or two things standing in their way, picking a date will usually give them what they need to set things in order. Offering a choice between two positives is a good approach. *"We are planning baptisms on October 1 and 22. Which date is best for you?" "Would you prefer for you or your husband to be baptized first?"* You can only get decisions if you ask for them. So look for the signals and when the light turns green move forward.

Decision Texts

1. *This step will cost me too much.* Luke 18:28-30; Matthew 16:24–27

2. *I can't leave my church.* Revelation 18:4; John 10:14-16, 27; 12:42, 43; Matthew 7:21–27

3. *I will lose my job if I keep the Sabbath.* Matthew 16:25, 26; 1 Timothy 4:8; Psalm 119:72

4. *I can't make a living if I keep the Sabbath.* Matthew 6:25, 26, 33; Psalm 37:3, 25; 34:10; Deuteronomy 30:19, 20; Job 23:10-12

5. *My family is opposing me.* Matthew 10:34-37; Luke 14:25-27; Luke 12:49-53

6. *There is something I can't give up.* (Alcohol, tobacco, jewelry, etc.) Matthew 6:24; 13:45, 46; Luke 14:33; Matthew 19:16-22

7. *I am afraid.* Isaiah 41:10: Psalm 119:57–60

8. *Not now.* Proverbs 27:1; 2 Corinthians 6:2; Hebrews 3:13; Isaiah 55:6; Genesis 6:3; Acts 22:16

9. *I am waiting for my spouse* (or friend) *so we can do it together.* Ezekiel 14:20; 18:20; Romans 14:12

10. *Some things are not clear yet.* John 12:35; Psalm 119:105, 60; John 13:6–8

11. *God is love. He will save me anyway.* John 14:15; 8:31, 32; 1 John 5:2, 3

12. *I don't believe I need to join a church.* Acts 2:47; 1 Corinthians 12:12, 13; Ephesians 1:22, 23

13. *I am too old to change my ways.* Matthew 20:6, 7; Genesis 6:3

14. *I will wait until the Spirit convinces me.* Acts 5:32; John 16:13; Psalm 119:142

Discuss, Learn, Apply

1. How can you recognize the golden moment a person is under conviction to make a decision for Jesus?

2. What role do the heart and mind (reason) play in the decision making process?

3. Give examples of how you can appeal to a person's heart to follow Jesus.

4. Why is it important to give people answers straight from the Bible as they are making a decision?

Chapter 23
DIP AND DASH EVANGELISM

As you follow the principles taught in this book, you will undoubtedly experience the joy of seeing someone commit their life to Jesus in baptism. But what will you do with your new babe in Christ after they're baptized?

In many churches, freshly-baptized members are hung out to drip-dry while the people who led them to Jesus quickly move on to find the next convert to dunk. This is what I call "dip and dash evangelism."

Up until this point, the potential new member has been the recipient of abundant attention. After they officially join the church, however, there is a drastic change. The weekly Bible studies, visits from the pastor, and the evangelistic meetings that filled their evenings, all disappear to leave a gaping chasm. They may question what they did wrong to be dumped like this!

Where is the body of Christ to help nurture the new babe in Christ? It should not surprise us, but with no special plan to help new members grow in Christ, they will often slip out the church's back door within a few months.

This is not Winsome Witnessing! Your mission as a soul-winner is not complete when you hear the gurgling sounds of the water drain from the baptistery. In fact, like a parent who has just delivered a child, your work is just beginning!

Why don't more people comprehend this? Perhaps it is because we misunderstand the mission Jesus entrusted to us in Matthew 28. Somehow, we have accepted the mistaken notion that the grand purpose of the church and evangelism is simply to baptize people.

This may be new to you, but baptizing new converts is not our ultimate objective. Our purpose is much more comprehensive. Let me explain how a crucial misunderstanding of the Great Commission could be spoiling your church's evangelistic efforts.

In Matthew 28:18-20, Jesus uses four verbs to describe the church's mission. The first verb is to "*go* to all the world." As a denomination, Seventh-day Adventists are good at "going." We take the message of Christ to the world through mission work, church planting, using media such as Hope Channel, the Internet, radio, and print. On a more personal level, we may witness to our neighbors, become missionaries, or financially support God's worldwide work.

Adventists take "going" seriously. It is the reason we are a global movement today. Yet, while establishing gospel centers in every country is vitally important, it isn't enough to fulfill Jesus' ultimate aim in the Great Commission. If it were, then Jesus' would have returned a long time ago. While "going to the world" is part of the church's mission, it is not the ultimate goal. Rather, it is an important step along the path.

Another verb in the Great Commission is to *baptize* people "in the name of the Father and of the Son and of the Holy Spirit." Many focus on this part of Jesus' command and see baptism as the crucial goal to fulfill the mission Jesus gave His church. They reason, isn't this why we go to the world with the gospel—to see people be baptized?

But again, baptism is not the final target Jesus had in mind. If it were, there wouldn't be any problem with dip and dash evangelism. While baptism is another step in the journey towards Christ's goal, it is still only a step.

A third verb Jesus uses is *teach*. In addition to "going and baptizing," Jesus commands, "teach them to observe all things that I have commanded you." Teaching is essential to fulfilling the Great Commission. We "go" to teach God's life-transforming truth, and people respond to learning God's will by being baptized. But teaching is still only a means to an end. It is not the final purpose Jesus commands us to achieve.

This leaves only one more verb to consider and that is to "*make* disciples." This last verb is often overlooked because of an inadequate translation in some Bibles rendering this as "teach all nations." A more accurate translation of the text, however, is "make disciples of all nations."

It is within this fourth verb that we find the true purpose of God's church. We exist to make disciples. We are not here to check off countries on some celestial list or to compile impressive baptismal statistics. As good as these may be, our purpose is much more eternal. According to the Great Commission, the real reason we go, teach, and baptize is so we can make disciples for Christ.

Therefore, you need to help every new person you lead to Christ become a full-fledged disciple. One of the best ways to accomplish this is to take them with you on your next Bible study. Better yet, have them give the studies to one of their contacts and you coach them. By helping new members grow in their walk with Christ you will avoid the dangers of the dip and dash evangelism model.

In order to experience eternal kingdom growth, your church needs to have "making disciples" as its goal. If it doesn't, you can win souls all day long, but they are not going to stay and help build God's cause. Instead, your church will continue to feel a drafty breeze blowing through its empty pews as new members and young adults exit the church through the open back door. The good news is that you can close the back door. In our next chapter, I will show you how as we explore what it means to make disciples.

Discuss, Learn, Apply

1. List the four verbs Jesus used to describe the mission of the church in Matthew 28:18-20.

2. How do going, teaching, and baptizing contribute to the mission to make disciples?

3. How would you describe the main goal of your local church?

4. Does your church need to refocus or change its goal? How?

Chapter 24
CALLED TO MAKE DISCIPLES

*I*n the Great Commission, Jesus commanded us to go, teach, and baptize people so that we can make disciples for His glory. The going, teaching, and baptizing are not ends in themselves, but are the means to the end. It is vitally important to understand that the reason we go, teach, and baptize is to make disciples. This is our God-given mission. And it needs to happen with everyone you lead to Christ and in the lives of the young people growing up in the church.

But what does it practically mean to "make disciples"? How are we to do this? And, how can you know when you have successfully accomplished it?

Let's answer these questions by discovering the biblical meaning for "disciple." Probably the most concise definition can be found in Jesus' description recorded in Matthew 10:25, "It is enough for a disciple to be like his teacher and a servant like his master."

The word "disciple" literally means a "learner" or "student." In this text, Jesus says that disciples are to be trained to become like their master or teacher. Therefore, the entire purpose of the church—the reason we go to all the world teaching the gospel, and baptizing people—is to help people become like Jesus, their Master. We want lost people to experience the love and power of Jesus as their Savior and Master. And as they do, the gospel will wholly transform their lives, making them more like Jesus in godly character.

Listen to this description of the amazing miracle of spiritual regeneration: "The more man views his Saviour and becomes acquainted with Him, the more he will become assimilated to His image and work the works of Christ" (*Testimonies for the Church*, Vol. 4, p. 488).

When we lead a person to Jesus, our long-term goal is to help them learn how to walk with Him as a fully committed follower. This is why we don't abandon new converts after their baptism. Instead, we engage them in a continued series of study and mentoring to help them learn how to reflect Jesus' character in their lives.

Let's be clear. Our purpose as soul-winners is not to corral a large group of new members to warm a pew on Sabbath morning while remaining prisoners the rest of the week to bad temper, selfishness, and ungodliness. Jesus accepts sinners where they are, but He doesn't leave them where He finds them. Rather, He patiently works with us to provide instruction, correction, and faith-building experiences. His goal is to make us "complete, thoroughly equipped for every good work" (2 Timothy 3:16, 17).

As Winsome Witnesses we will patiently and lovingly help new converts discover the abundant life Jesus has for them. Anything short of this misses the mark of what it means to be a Christian. God has called us to help make disciples who reflect Jesus' character. "He proposes to make us like Himself, true in every purpose, feeling, and thought—true in heart, soul, and life. This is Christianity" (*Testimonies for the Church*, vol. 5, p. 235).

This is what your church is called to do in the lives of its new members. And it is your personal mission as a witness for Jesus. You are to help people fall so in love with Jesus that your student begins assimilating the characteristics of their Teacher, Jesus.

I tell my children, "You are a Gibbs." What I mean is that there are certain standards and characteristics we cherish in our family. In fact, I have written down the character qualities that I want to help my children develop. I use this list to pray for my children and to direct my parenting. My goal is to so imprint these characteristics in their lives that it becomes natural for them to reflect these "Gibbs" qualities wherever they go.

God also has a list of character qualities that He seeks to develop in each of His children. You can find these "spiritual growth goals" in Ephesians 4. As you read this list, think of it as skills and qualities that you will help every new believer develop.

- "Equipping of the saints for the work of *ministry*." (v. 12)
- "Till we all come to the *unity* of the faith." (v. 13)
- "And of the *knowledge of the Son of God*." (v. 13)
- "To the *measure* of the stature of the fullness of Christ." (v. 13)
- "That we should no longer be...carried about with every wind of *doctrine*." (v. 14)
- "*Speaking the truth in love*." (v. 15)
- "Every part *does its share*." (v. 16)

Note that these seven personal spiritual goals are presented in Scripture as the result of the church exercising its spiritual gifts to make disciples. In other words, the reason we pastor, do Sabbath School, Pathfinders, deacon work, or any other job in the church is to "equip the saints for the work of ministry," to bring them into "the unity of the faith and of the knowledge of the Son of God," to help them learn accurate biblical doctrine, and acquire the other three qualities mentioned. These are the reasons we have church positions and ministries. It is not just because we've always done it this way or the conference tells us we need to fill these positions. We are here to make disciples—people who are growing in these seven areas.

We can add to this list three additional qualities to make a total of ten. You'll find them in the description of God's last day people in Revelation 14:12.

- "Here is the *patience* of the saints." ("This calls for *patient endurance* on behalf of the saints." New International Version.)

- "Here are those who *keep the commandments* of God and the *faith of Jesus.*"

We need to help new members learn how to patiently endure as good soldiers of Christ, how to have patience with the saints, and how to keep God's commandments by faith and loving devotion rather than by a desire to earn their salvation.

Can you imagine what your church will be when it trains every new member to acquire these ten characteristics and skills? It will be powerful! On the other hand, it is a sad fact that unless you intentionally help your new members grow as Christians in these ten character qualities, you will either lose them or they will be mediocre believers. This is why you must have a plan to disciple every new member, whether they be an adult or young person. Anything less than this not only misses the very purpose God organized the church, but it does an eternal disservice to the new converts.

Discuss, Learn, Apply

1. According to Jesus in Matthew 10:25, what is a disciple?

2. According to *Testimonies for the Church, Volume 5,* page 235, what does Jesus propose to do in our lives?

3. Choose at least two of the ten character qualities and skills found in Ephesians 4 and Revelation 14:12 and describe practical ways how you would help someone grow in these areas.

Chapter 25
NOBODY MEETS SOMEBODY

S omeone once quipped, When all else fails, read the directions. I have learned the hard way that there is always a terrible price to pay when I don't carefully follow the instructions that come with a product.

Once, I was in a hurry to get a house repair done before leaving later that day for an extended international trip. My job was to seal leaking air ducts that were increasing my electrical bills. With summer arriving in a few weeks, I needed to fix the problem before leaving town.

I chose a spray foam insulation to seal the holes and gaps in my ductwork. It is a product that I used in the past, but unknown to me the formula had changed. The new version contains a very sticky adhesive that is next to impossible to remove. Perhaps this is why the manufacturer put on the can in bold letters: WEAR GLOVES WHEN USING THIS PRODUCT.

I saw the instructions before starting, but I was in a hurry to get the project completed. Plus, I had used the product before and never had a problem with cleaning the foam off my hands. Consequently, I ignored the bold warning.

An hour later, as I rushed to seal the last hole, I became concerned about the time. I needed to clean up, pack, and rush to the airport to catch my flight. This is when I noticed my fingers and hands, now covered in the spray foam, were terribly stained with a dark, bubble gum-like substance. "No problem," I thought. "I will just wash it off and be on my way."

I soon discovered that no amount of soap and water could remove it. With the clock ticking, I was getting desperate. My hands looked terrible. Besides, they were so sticky, if I shook someone's hand they would be permanently glued to me!

While I ultimately did remove the mess with gasoline and lots of scrubbing, the lesson *stuck* with me: always follow directions.

Similarly, the church has gotten itself into a mess by neglecting to follow Jesus' instruction to make disciples. We must quickly clean this up before we can exit this world for an extended journey into eternity. To do this, we need to focus our energies on implementing a disciple-making process for every new member.

Why haven't we seen a stronger disciple-making emphasis in the church? Perhaps the answer can be found in the following counsel:

"Some ministers and churches are so desirous of securing an increase of numbers that they do not bear faithful testimony against unchristian habits and practices. Those who accept the truth are not taught that they cannot safely be worldlings in conduct while they are Christians in name. ... Little self-denial or self-sacrifice is required in order to put on a form of godliness and to have one's name enrolled upon the church book. Hence many join the church without first becoming united to Christ. In this Satan triumphs. Such converts are his most efficient agents. They serve as decoys to other souls" (*Testimonies for the Church*, vol. 5, p. 172).

While it is imperative that we avoid destructive legalistic and judgmental attitudes, we still need to patiently and faithfully teach people how to make a full surrender to Jesus. If people are robbed of a true conversion experience because of our unfaithfulness, they could very well become Satan's "most efficient agents" within the church!

This reminds me of the story of a revival in a small town. After the meetings concluded, the pastors of the three participating congregations got together for breakfast to share how the revival blessed each of their churches.

The Methodist minister excitedly told his fellow pastors, "The revival worked out great for us! We gained four new families." With a bit of sanctified pride, the Baptist preacher crowed, "We did better than that! We gained six new families." In the silence of the next moment, all eyes turned to the third pastor to hear how his church fared. They noticed the Presbyterian pastor had a little smile twitching at the corners of his mouth. Eyes twinkling, he announced, "Well, we did even better than that! We got rid of our 10 biggest troublemakers!"

Churches that don't grow can often point to members standing in the way who have not been discipled. These members are the tail wagging the dog. They manipulate the entire congregation by insisting that everything be done their way.

Unfortunately, I've seen churches grow only after they've had a few good funerals. (You don't want to be the problem that has to be buried.) Better yet, if a funeral is needed to fix things, it should be the watery grave kind—rebaptism. The best option, however, is to follow God's plan from the beginning—establish a disciple making ethos in your church where every member commits to being discipled and to participate in discipling others.

Neglecting disciple making is dangerous to healthy church growth and life. "The accession of members who have not been renewed in heart and reformed in life is a source of weakness to the church. This fact is often ignored" (*Testimonies for the Church*, vol. 5, p. 172).

The good news is that weak churches can become strong and healthy when they embrace the idea that their business is to cooperate with the Holy Spirit to change lives. This is why you must not be content to simply baptize people and feel your mission is complete. "Our efforts are not to cease because public meetings have been discontinued for a time… the new converts will need to be instructed by faithful teachers of God's Word, that they may increase in a knowledge and love of the truth, and may grow to the full stature of men and women in Christ Jesus. They must now be surrounded by the influences most favorable to spiritual growth" (*Evangelism*, p. 337).

Making disciples requires you to very intentionally commit to this wonderful work with every new person you bring to Christ. Yet, consider what happens much too often in our churches: "Our Redeemer throws souls into the arms of the church, for them to care for unselfishly and train for heaven, and thus be coworkers with Him. But the church too often thrusts them away, upon the devil's battlefield. One member will say, 'It is not my duty,' and then bring up some trifling excuse. 'Well,' says another, 'neither is it my duty;' and finally it is nobody's duty, and the soul is left uncared for to perish. It is the duty of every Christian to engage in this self-denying, self-sacrificing enterprise. Cannot God return into His granaries and increase their flocks, so that instead of loss there shall be increase?" (*Testimonies for the Church*, Vol. 2, p. 331).

Whose job is it to train new members to be disciples? In the foregoing church, it is "nobody's" duty. Look around your church. Do you have a member named "Nobody"? Probably not, even though you may hear several people lament, "nobody is doing it." If someone ever shows up at your church with the name of Nobody, tell them to beware—they are going to be overloaded with church jobs.

Because "Nobody" is making disciples in your church, I am challenging you to be "Somebody." As somebody who is committed to truly winning souls, not just for time but for eternity, you can be used by God to disciple new believers. You will experience the positive influence healthy new members will make in your church. So, let's be "somebody" and stop paying the terrible price for "nobody's" neglect to make disciples.

Discuss, Learn, Apply

1. According to *Testimonies for the Church, Volume 5*, page 172, why don't more churches and ministers focus on making true disciples for Jesus?

2. What can you do to help new converts grow in Christ according to *Evangelism*, page 337?

3. How do you feel about being "somebody" who disciples new members? What next step can you take to be this "somebody"?

Chapter 26
RECIPE FOR SUCCESS

I became a Christian through a series of Bible lectures on prophecy sponsored by the Seventh-day Adventist Church. God found me at a very receptive time. I had recently graduated from school and was contemplating my future. That's when I recalled meeting a man in my childhood who introduced me to the concept that God has revealed the future to mankind in His Word.

Looking back, I can see how God used this man to plant this seed of truth in my mind. It led me to rationalize, "If I can understand what God says about the future of this world, then I will know how to plan my future." At the time, I had no interest in becoming a Christian. In fact, I was studying Buddhism and practicing an ungodly lifestyle. Even still, prophecy interested me and I attended the Adventist meetings on prophecy.

The meetings turned out to be truly life-changing. Not only did I learn about last day events, but I discovered that God has a plan for my life. Most importantly, I met Jesus and accepted Him as my Lord and Savior. He has been leading me ever since into an exciting life of ministry and much more.

When I was baptized, I am sure that no one in the church that day dreamed how God was going to lead this seventeen-year-old kid. By all appearances, I didn't look like a budding pastor, evangelist, or television ministry leader. I had long hair down my back and rode a motorcycle to church. My speech was unrefined and my manners were far from Christian.

However, this didn't discourage Dickey, the personal ministries leader in my new church. A week or two after my baptism, he invited me to tag along with him to visit people who attended the Bible seminar but had not made decisions to join the church. Little did he know he was being used that day to start me on a lifelong path of evangelism.

Dickey continued to minister to me with invitations to his house each Sabbath afternoon where I was introduced to vegetarian food and how to keep the Sabbath. Soon, I was spending Friday nights and all day Sabbath at Dickey and Deborah's home. We spent many hours studying the Bible and talking about the faith, as I transitioned from one lifestyle to another.

Shortly after this, God used several others to disciple me. I met Robert Wagley and Steve Vail at camp meeting one month after my baptism.

The three of us grew up just a few miles from each other in Baton Rouge, Louisiana, but since they were a few years older, we had not met before. When they first saw me at camp meeting, I still looked like a hippie. That didn't stop them from inviting me to stay with them at their friends Don and Karen Ryder's house during camp meeting. When I accepted their generous invitation, I didn't realize that a relationship was being formed that would bless me to this day.

Over the next several years, they, along with their wives Peggy and Connie, taught me the importance of daily devotional time, how to study the Spirit of Prophecy, the call to witness for Christ, healthful living, and a whole lot more. There were many others, like O.J. and Millie Mills, whom God used in a huge way to grow me as a new Adventist Christian. In fact, it would take another page to mention each person by name.

Here is the point that I want you to get from my story: *people disciple people.* I would not be the Christian I am today if these people had not reached out and allowed me to share their life and passion for God. This is disciple making in its purest sense. And it is what God wants you to do for the new members who join your church.

But just how are you to disciple people? The answer can be found in this statement where the five ingredients of good disciple making are described. "*Care* should be exercised to *educate* young converts. They are *not to be left to themselves*, to be led astray by false presentations, to walk in a false way. Let the watchmen be constantly on guard, lest souls shall be beguiled by soft words and fair speech and sophistry. *Teach* faithfully all that *Christ has commanded.* Everyone who receives Christ is to be *trained to act some part in the great work* to be accomplished in our world" (*Evangelism*, p. 367).

Care. If your church is committed to the Great Commission, you will care about making disciples. Your care will be expressed in laying specific plans to disciple new members. You will not leave disciple making to chance, because you care for people and their eternal welfare.

Educate. You will also recognize that discipling new members is an educational *process*—it takes time. New members don't learn everything overnight. One Sabbath evening, shortly after my baptism, I returned to church for the evening service. Dickey and some others asked me how my afternoon had gone. With abundant enthusiasm, I described how my family had enjoyed a crawfish "boil" (that is a "meal" for everyone not from Louisiana). Then I announced, "Those were the best crawfish I have ever eaten." Everyone grew quiet for a moment and then the conversation continued on something else.

Wisely, no one lectured me on the perils of eating unclean foods, saying, "Son, don't you know better than to eat unclean foods? Didn't they teach you this before you joined the church?" Instead, Dickey invited me to his house every Sabbath for lunch and afternoon fellowship—effectively taking care of the crawfish problem!

We need to be patient with new members. They need time to fully understand how Bible truth is to integrate with every aspect of their life. I had studied about clean and unclean foods prior to baptism. I also went through a baptismal class that reviewed it in detail. But somehow, I had not connected the dots in my head.

The truth that I learned in the evangelistic meetings became practical, however, when people spent time with me. That's when I saw truth in action. They taught me by precept and example how to live the biblical lifestyle.

Befriend—don't leave new members to themselves. One excellent way to stay close to new members is to pair them with an existing member to mentor them. The pastor can introduce the mentor by saying, "John and Mary, we are so happy you have joined our church. We want you to get the most out of being a church member. To help you grow in your walk with Jesus, we have asked Michael and Susan to be your hosts in our church. We think you have a lot in common and that you will enjoy their fellowship." Of course, if you are the person who gave them Bible studies, you will definitely be at least one of their mentors.

In fact, it is vital that new members develop *multiple* meaningful relationships in your church. This is one of the most important factors in their spiritual growth. In the context of safe relationships, people will open their heart to learn how to walk with Jesus as their eternal friend.

Teach faithfully all that Christ has commanded. We already said that becoming a disciple is an educational process. Once a person joins the church, they need to go back through another series of Bible studies. It can even be the same material that first attracted them or it can be something new. I prefer to do this study in a small group so that the new member can interact and learn from others as they form more friendships. Be sure to also involve your new members in regular Sabbath School attendance. If you have a large influx of members after an evangelistic meeting, you should seriously consider a special class for them. It will go a long way to encourage regular Sabbath School attendance, personal devotional habits, and church friendships.

Train to act some part in the great work. This is what Dickey and others did for me when I first committed my life to Christ. Do not wait for your new members to either become perfect or lose their zeal for Christ before you get them involved. Get them involved in ministries that are low stress and where they can safely develop healthy relationships. If they have special gifts, begin to involve them where they can use their God-given talents to bless others. They may not do things the traditional way the first time around, but give them time and coaching and you will see a wonderful return on your trust.

One of the most useful things you can do is involve your new members in giving Bible studies with you. New members have family and friends who are curious about their new faith. Teach them how to turn their family's questions into sit-down Bible studies. You can coach them how to give the study by going with them. Why not give them their very own copy of *Winsome Witnessing* to read? If someone had given me a book like this, perhaps I wouldn't have made so many of the embarrassing mistakes I've told you about and more souls would have been won.

As you *care, educate, befriend, teach,* and *train* for ministry, you will also keep your eye on helping your new members develop the ten character qualities and skills mentioned earlier. Be sure to enlist your new members in this process by inviting them to commit to spiritual development. Explain to them what it means to be a disciple and share how you are there to help them enjoy their new found faith in this world and throughout eternity.

As you win souls, you have a wonderful opportunity to create a disciple making culture in your church where everyone is committed to personal growth in Jesus Christ. Not only will you find that your new members stay in the church, but you will also see your church become a vibrant body of believers living out what it means to be Jesus' disciples.

For more information and resources on making disciples visit www. HopeNETonline.org . You can also visit www.GrowingFruitfulDisciples.com .

Discuss, Learn, Apply

1. List the five ingredients for making disciples according to *Evangelism*, page 367.

2. Which of these five ingredients seems the most important to you? Explain.

3. Is there someone you are discipling or that you can disciple right now? Who is it and what are you doing, or will do, with them as a result of reading these chapters on disciple making?

Chapter 27
LET'S GET STARTED

I trust you have benefited from reading this book with not only practical information, but to be inspired to think witnessing is something you can do. You may be feeling like you need to read it several more times before you are ready to witness or give studies. Please don't do this. You can consult these pages from time to time for help in a particular area, but to learn how to witness you really need to just jump in and start. This is how everyone learns.

When I first began, I thought someone else was going to teach me. The evangelist I worked with told me that Bob would go on the studies with me. I took this to mean Bob would train me. As Bob and I stood at the very first door, I said to him, *"I sure am glad you're here to teach me because I would be petrified right now. I want to see how you do this."* With alarm ringing in his voice Bob squeaked, *"Did you say, 'I am teaching you?' I thought you were going to teach me!"* Apparently Bob didn't know any more than I did about what we were doing. But here we were standing at a door with people ready to open it and find two dumbstruck mutes staring at them. We were in the water and it was time to either dog paddle or drown. When the door swung open, Bob was speechless. I stammered something that time has mercifully erased from my memory, but it apparently sounded good enough to at least Bob. He smiled confidently as he swaggered away from the home after our visit. *"Wow! You did really well at that."* I think anything would have qualified as "really well" at that point. Its funny how I was usually the one that got to do the talking from there on.

Lessons and training are great. It is good to get as much information as you can on witnessing, but there comes a time when you will not learn anything else unless you get out there and start dancing to the sound of your quavering voice, knocking knees and thumping heart. I can promise you the Spirit of God will be right there to help you every step along the way. Better than my promise, here is one that is inspired. We read it earlier in these pages but let's read it again—this time much more deliberately:

"He who begins with a little knowledge, in a humble way, and tells what he knows, while seeking diligently for further knowledge, will find the whole heavenly treasure awaiting his demand. The more he seeks to impart light, the more light he will receive. The more one tries to explain the Word of God to others, with a love for souls, the plainer it becomes to himself. The more we use our knowledge and exercise our powers, the more knowledge and power we shall have" (*Christ's Object Lessons*, p. 354).

Do you have a "little knowledge?" Certainly you do. You've made it this far through the book, so you qualify in God's sight. (Sorry I didn't tell you this before you became accountable.) Are you humble? Most likely. If not, maybe you should go back and read some more and see how truly dependent we are on God. Now here is the kicker—will you tell what you know? You don't have to know much. Remember, only a "little knowledge" is all that is needed to begin.

Will you "seek to impart light" and "try to explain the Word of God to others?" In the beginning the light you impart and your attempted explanations might feel like false starts. But as you try and as you seek, you will see the promise of these words come true. The whole treasure of heaven's resources of wisdom and ability will be opened to your understanding. The truths of the Bible will become plainer to you than ever before. You will hear in your heart the Spirit of God utter the very words that you need to speak. You will gain a sense of confidence that you never knew you could ever possess. This and so much more is all yours! God has promised. It cannot fail. And all you need to do is start.

You can't afford to do any less. You owe it to yourself. You will find the spiritual power you always knew must be out there somewhere. Your family needs you to do this. Your example will help them come closer to God. Lost people are hoping you will do it. They are patiently waiting for someone who knows the very truth they long to learn. And they don't care that you're not an expert. They just want to know what you know.

Most important, God is longing for you to start. He wants to speak to you in ways that He couldn't before because easy chair religion has blocked Him. He wants to show you what it is like to really be filled with the Spirit. Fresh and vibrant insights into Christ, He waits to give you. And then there are the multitudes of lost men and women, boys and girls that He loves so much. He wants to hug them in heaven. But He first needs you to bring them there.

Will you try? Will you do it for Jesus? I am praying you will.

"Father in heaven, I know that witnessing and giving studies is something that frightens many of your children. Others want to do it but they are too busy or don't know where to start. O Lord, I pray for the person reading this right now. I don't know what the devil will use to keep them from reaching out to the lost. I do know they

have an interest in being used by you. So please break every hold the enemy may have that will prevent them from starting. Even this very week, Lord, I ask that you will give them a witnessing experience. Let them feel the joy that comes when we share your love with another. Enable them to get a study with one of your seeking sheep that is trying to make their way to your fold. And O God, I pray for my friend that one day soon you will come and we will ride back in the clouds to heaven to stand on the sea of glass together. May they find that as they lift their happy voices in praise to you, they are looking into the smiling faces of people they have introduced to Jesus. This is my prayer in the all wonderful and merciful name of your Son. Amen."

Discuss, Learn, Apply

1. What has been most helpful for you as you have read this book?

2. God wants to use you to lead people to Jesus. Are you willing to accept this challenge? How do you feel about this decision?

3. Write down the next steps that you will take to follow God's call and include target dates.

APPENDIX

Media Survey

"Hello, _____ (name of person). I am _____ representing _____ (either Hope Channel, 3ABN, Amazing Facts, It Is Written, Voice of Prophecy, Faith for Today, Breath of Life, Christian Lifestyle, Quiet Hour, Signs of the Times magazine). (Hold a brochure with the picture of the speaker if you have it). (If you have the station information and time for the broadcast ministry: We are on here at _____ .) *I am visiting people who have heard our broadcast (or received the magazine) to ask them to help us with a brief survey of three questions. This survey will help us determine which topics interest people. May I have a few minutes of your time to ask you these questions for our survey?"* (While going through the survey, be sure to briefly discuss and comment on the reason for each question and discuss each of their answers.)

1. *"How often do you watch/listen to the broadcast?"* (For *Signs* magazine: *"How long have you received Signs magazine?"*) Regularly _____ Occasionally _____ Seldom _____ How many years? _____

2. *"Which of the following topics most interest you?"* (Helps us know what programs the community is interested in.) Circle areas of interest.

   a. Health (low cholesterol cooking, stress reduction, quitting smoking, exercise, etc.)

   b. Family (marriage, husband/wife communication, parent/ child relations, etc.)

   c. The Christian Life (prayer, Bible study, faith, salvation, handling temptation, etc.)

   d. Bible Prophecy (last-day events, fulfilled prophecy, Daniel and the Revelation, etc.)

   e. Archaeology (How discoveries in the Middle East confirm the Bible.)

3. *"Which one of the topics you just mentioned has the highest interest to you?"*

4. *"Thank you for helping us with this survey. Your answers help us know which topics to use when developing community programs. We*

appreciate your participation and would like to invite you to enjoy a free Bible study course on Bible prophecy and other interesting Bible topics. (Show the lesson[s]). Hand them a copy for them to look at.) *If you are interested in them, I would be happy for you to have them.* (If they are interested, give them the first study guide. Explain that you will give them a brief study of the next week's lesson.) *You are really going to enjoy these studies!* (Make an appointment to return next week to receive their completed guide and to give them the next lesson along with the brief Bible study overview you will provide.) *Is this a good time for me to bring your next lessons?"*

"Thank you so much for your helpful answers to our survey. This information will be very useful to us as we plan future ministry. I appreciate your time. Have a wonderful day!"

Church Visitors Canvass

Everyone who visits your church can be visited using the following approach. Many of these visits will result in Bible studies.

1. Have a way to get complete addresses from all visitors on Sabbath morning.

2. These addresses need to be given immediately to those who will make the visits. It is best to visit the people Monday or Tuesday after they have worshiped with you.

3. Bring copies of the Bible study guides on your visit.

4. When you go to the door, smile and say, *"Hi, John, my name is _____ . I worship at the local Seventh-day Adventist Church. I am out making brief visits with those who worshiped with us this past Saturday. I have a special gift I'd like to leave with you. Do you have a moment? I can't stay long."*

5. Bring the prospect a gift wrapped copy of a book like *Happiness Digest* or *Your Friends the Adventists* or some other short helpful book on a neutral topic. Do not use full message books like *The Great Controversy,* and avoid very thick books. Do not give anything with a summary of all our beliefs.

6. Visit briefly with the people. Be very gracious and genuinely friendly. Give them your gift. Express how you appreciated them attending. Ask them how they found everything. Were they comfortable? Were they able to become acquainted with anyone? The **FORT** conversation is a good outline to use for your visit.

7. Find a point to offer the free Bible study guides. Here is a sample script:

   "Has anyone offered you our free Bible study guides, yet? I have a copy of them if you'd like to see it. They are on. … If you like them I will be happy to leave it with you. (The script in the *Something Wonderful for You Card* canvass on *"About the Study Guides, How The Program Works, and Set the Appointment"* is perfect to use at this stage.)

8. You usually don't want to stay longer than 15-30 minutes. Have prayer and say you look forward to seeing them again.

Former and Inactive Members Survey

"More than a million Adventists no longer attend their church. The Adventist Church is now trying to discover the reason. Our local church is interested in improving its ministry. Please help us make our church better by briefly answering the following questions:

1. *"How did you become a Seventh-day Adventist?"* (When and how were you baptized, who encouraged you, who baptized you, and how did you feel about your baptism?)

2. *"How long did you attend church regularly?"*

3. *"Who were your friends when you were in church?"*

4. *"How long has it been since you attended church regularly?"*

5. *"What do you consider the chief reason you no longer attend church?"*

6. *"Did you have a personal conflict with any member?"* (Such as with a pastor, principal, teacher, or other.) *If so, please explain.*

7. *"What would you need to come back to church?"*

8. *"May I ask you a personal question? If you were to die tonight, or if Jesus were to return, would you have the assurance of eternal life?"* (Use the dialogue on how to lead a person to Christ.)

9. (If not) *"May I share with you how you can have this assurance?"*

10. *"We have a set of simple Bible study lessons that I think you would enjoy. May I share them with you?"*

Community Religious Survey

"I have volunteered to take a brief survey today asking people their opinions on community spiritual and religious issues. It is only five questions long. I am not selling anything and this will only take a few minutes. Your help would be appreciated. Could you help me with these five questions?"

1. *"What is your church or religious preference?"*
   a. Christian _____ Which church or denomination? _____
   b. Catholic ____ c. Jew ____ d. Hindu ____ e. Buddhism _____
   f. Islam ____ g. Other ____ h. None _____
2. *"Do you attend a place of worship?"* _____
3. *"How often do you attend?"* a. Consistently ____
   b. Moderately ___ c. Almost Never ___ d. Do Not Attend ___
4. *"Do you believe that if the Bible were read and followed it would help people solve some of the problems they face today? Why or Why not?"*
5. *"Suppose four seminars were being held in our town tonight at the same time and you were going to attend one. Which one of the following would you attend?"*
   a. Health (low cholesterol cooking, stress reduction, quitting smoking, exercise, etc.)
   b. Family (marriage, husband/wife communication, parent/child relations, etc.)
   c. The Christian Life (prayer, Bible study, faith, salvation, handling temptation, etc.)
   d. Bible Prophecy (last-day events, prophecy for our days, Daniel and the Revelation, etc.)
6. *"Thank you for participating in our survey. Your answers help us know the religious preferences of people and their opinions. This will help as community events are planned in the future. As a token of my thanks here is a free pamphlet I hope you enjoy that deals with _____ ."* (Give a free pamphlet on an interesting neutral topic such as salvation, freedom from guilt, etc.)

"I also have some free Bible study reading guides on _____ . *They are designed for busy people and they cover Bible subjects such as* _____ . *Do these free guides interest you?"* (If the answer is positive then say, *"Fine. May I take a moment to explain them to you?"* The script in the *Something Wonderful for You* Card canvass on *"About the Study Guides, How The Program Works, and Set the Appointment"* can be used at this stage with the exception that you might need to go soft on offering these as in the home sit down studies. If the people seem to be especially open then you can do this, otherwise start with a drop off study and then try to transition later into sit down studies once they have become comfortable with you.)

Circle of Influence Canvasses

Everyone has a circle of persons whom they influence. This circle includes family, friends, neighbors, co-workers, and casual acquaintances. God has provided these relationships for a purpose— that we might be a winning influence. Here is a simple approach to help you lead them to Christ through Bible studies. Memorize any of these short canvasses and adapt it to suit your particular situation.

1. *"I have just come across some interesting Bible study guides that you might be interested in. They cover Bible prophecy and other interesting topics. I've wanted to do them myself, but was hoping to find someone to share them with as well. I'd like to give you a couple of the lessons if they sound interesting to you."* (Show them the studies if you have them on hand. Set a time to meet with them once a week to go over the lessons together.)

2. *"I am currently taking a class to help me learn the Bible better. I enrolled with the desire to grow in my personal understanding of the Bible and am really learning a lot and enjoying it. Part of the course involves sharing the Bible with others. A special set of Bible study guides have been designed for me to give to others. The guides are written so that people of all faiths can enjoy them. They are colorful, informative, and inspirational. They cover topics that are of interest to most people—If God is so good, why is the world so bad, What does the Bible have to say about our day, and many others. Do you think this is something that you can help me with?"* (Show them the study guides.)

3. If you are close to the beginning of an evangelistic series you could say, *"I recently heard about a seminar on Bible prophecy and how it relates to today that is coming to town soon. There are some Bible study*

guides that people are going through before the meetings. These studies will help me better understand the Bible and prepare for the meetings. If you have an interest in this type of thing, I'm happy to get you the free guides as well." (If they are interested you will try to turn this into a study that you do together.)

Letter to Family and Friends

Dear _____:

I am currently taking a class to help me learn the Bible better. I enrolled with the desire to grow in my personal understanding of the Bible and am really enjoying it and learning a lot.

Since part of my course involves helping other people to understand and enjoy the Bible, I am sending this letter to you and other friends and family who I thought might be interested in helping me.

A special set of Bible study guides, *Prophecies of Hope*, have been designed for me to give to others. The guides are written so that people of all faiths can enjoy them. They are colorful, informative, and inspirational. They cover topics that are of interest to most people—If God is so good, why is the world so bad; what does Bible prophecy have to say about our day; and many others. Do you think this is something you can help me with?

The *Prophecies of Hope* lessons are ideal for busy people. They are a free set of lessons that I will be able to give to you. You have a choice of how you will receive these guides. They can be done either through the mail or in person with me. Of course, the latter method really makes me learn the material and would be of special help to me.

I do hope that you will be able to take these simple Bible lessons and appreciate you considering this request. If you are unable at this time, I understand. I will phone you in a few days to see if you would enjoy these lessons and can help me with this class I am taking.

Sincerely,

Something Wonderful for You Card Canvass

A. General Recommendations

It is recommended that in most cases you don't phone before you make the first visit. Park in the street where possible. Don't block cars in the driveway. The spouse may return and find you in his/her parking space. At the door you need to RELAX and SMILE, SMILE, SMILE.

B. Script for *Something Wonderful for You* Cards.

There are six parts to this canvass. You don't need to memorize this word for word, but there are certain key phrases that you will find very helpful. If you will follow the order of this canvass you will find good success.

(1) The door

(2) The reason you are personally delivering it

(3) About the study guides

(4) Who they are studying with

(5) How the program works

(6) Set the appointment for next week.

1. The Door

"_____? (name of prospect). *My name is* _____ .

I am calling in response to the card you sent in for the free Bible study guides. (Show them their card.) *I just came by to drop your lessons off so you can start them. It will only take a couple of minutes to show you how to do them.*"

Go in the house. If they stall, tell them, "*You may have thought the information was going to come through the mail. But the reason we don't send it through the mail is because when many people get it they have questions about how to do the study-guides. It will only take a brief moment to explain exactly how to do the lessons.*" If you time this properly you might find the following body language will help you find an entrance. It sounds funny, but it does work. Back up from the door, break eye contact, glance at door handle, and shuffle your feet slightly.

2. The Reason You are Personally Delivering the Studies

If not covered at the door, after you are seated say,

"_____ ,(use their name) *a lot of people expect to get their studies through the mail.* (They will usually respond that this is what they thought.) *The reason for my bringing them is that when many people get the studies they don't know how to do them, so we deliver the free studies and in just a few moments explain exactly how to do them.*"

3. **About the Study Guides**

"Let me take a moment to show you how to do the studies. Here is how they look. (Hold up lesson 1.) The series is called..." "_____ (their name), many people have questions about the Bible and how it relates to their life today. Questions like 'What does the Bible have to say about current events? How do you find peace of mind in the midst of a world of turmoil? What does the future hold? How can you study the Bible to get true answers?' These lessons answer these questions. They're designed for busy people and only take minutes to do. Some people do them in one sitting, others take just a few questions a day and use it for their devotions."

Show how the lessons are in a question and answer format. *"The most attractive feature of these lessons is that they teach you how to interpret the Bible for yourself. Instead of telling you what to believe they show you how to use the Bible to interpret itself comparing all the different Bible texts on any given topic. This way you learn what the Bible has to say instead of reading about someone's opinions. Doesn't that sound good?*

"Here is how you do the study questions. You read the question and then look up the Bible reference in your own Bible. Then you will write the answer you find in the blank provided here."

Hand the open study guide to the person. And then in a relaxed manner move immediately into the next part of the script before the person has a chance to raise a question or to comment. You will answer who is sponsoring the studies. This is a part of the canvass that you will do well to memorize.

4. **Sponsors of the Studies**

"_____ (their name), you need to know who is sponsoring these studies and who you are studying with. There are many groups today that don't believe in the Bible and Jesus like most of us Christians. Let me assure you I am a Bible believing Christian who trusts Jesus Christ is God and the Son of God. He came to this world and lived a perfect life and then died on the cross to pay the penalty for our sins. Of course, I attend a church I am very proud of, and I don't mind sharing with you where I like to attend. But this isn't the purpose of our study together. I'd rather stay away from denominationalism for now. [If this is your case you can add: "I am a volunteer with a Christian ministry called _____ (you choose: Hope Channel, Amazing Facts, It Is Written, Voice of Prophecy, 3ABN, Faith for Today, etc.). They have a TV and

radio ministry for people of all faiths. Volunteers, like myself, choose not to make an issue of our personal denominational preferences since I believe God has people in every church.] The thing I like to focus on is teaching what the Bible says. I believe God has people in every church. My goal is to help people learn how to study the Bible for themselves. When I can show someone the tools to unravel the Bible's meaning then I feel like I've been successful. I want to ultimately become useless to my students. So when you are studying the Bible alone someday and you can't understand what you are reading, you will remember something you learned from our studies that will help you find the meaning. I feel that the most important thing for all Christians is to know their Bibles better, don't you? Are you comfortable with this?"

5. How the Program Works

"Let me explain to you how we do these studies. Each week I will check the lessons you've done and then give you a brief study of the next lesson you will do. People really appreciate this method and learn a lot from it." Compare the advantages of this method with the correspondence course method.

6. Set the Appointment for Next Week

"Would _____ (time and day) be a good time for me to stop by?"

General things to remember that you may need to tell the prospect:

"These lessons are to introduce people to the Bible. We are also sponsoring a public seminar that will cover more material in detail." The prospect is invited to attend. *"We conduct these Introductory lessons with the purpose of helping people understand the Bible for themselves."*

Do NOT give the prospect any other literature than the study guides. Do NOT give full-message books, pamphlets on the Sabbath, mark of the beast, etc. If they want information on a particular topic you are to encourage them to attend the public seminar.

Answers to Questions

Question: *"Who did you say you are with again?"*

Answer: "_____ , (name of prospect) *My name is _____ and I am with the Bible Reading Guides. I am calling in response to the card you sent in requesting your free Bible reading guides. (Show them their card.) I just came by to deliver your lessons. It will only take a brief moment to show you how to do the lessons. May I have a moment of your time?"*

Question: *"How much does this cost?"*

Answer: *"There is no cost now or at any time."*

Question: *"How did you get my name?"*

Answer: *"I received the card you sent requesting the studies."*

Question: *"I didn't send this card to you."*

Be aware that somebody other than the person to whom you are speaking may have sent the card for them. If this is the case, answer, *"Since I am already here may I have a brief moment of your time to explain our free Bible study guides. If you like them I will leave it with you."*

Question: *"Which church is sponsoring this?"*

Answer: *"I am a Christian volunteer working with. ..."* Remember, as a volunteer, you've been asked not to get into the denominationalism.

Question: *"I thought the studies were going to arrive by mail."*

Answer: *"Yes, some people do. This study is better than one through the mail. You don't have several weeks of delay waiting for the mail to return your corrected lesson."*

Resources—*Contact information for Media Ministries to obtain interest names and other resources:*

Adventist Media Center *(includes Breath of Life, It Is Written, and Voice of Prophecy)*
101 W Cochran St
Simi Valley, CA 93065
Phone:(805)955-7777
Fax:(805)955-7701
www.sdamedia.org

Amazing Facts
P.O. Box 1058
Roseville, CA 95678
Phone: (916) 434-3880
Fax: (916) 434-3889
www.amazingfacts.org

Hope Channel
PO Box 4000
Silver Spring, MD 20904
www.HopeTV.org
Visit www.HopeNETonline.org
for further evangelism training.

Prophecies of Hope

Prophecies of Hope is a set of 26 full-color, full-message Bible lessons developed by Gary Gibbs of Hope Channel. Holes punched for a 3-ring binder, along with a "fill-in-the-blanks" feature, make these lessons easy to use for busy lifestyles. Designed for use in evangelistic series, or as stand-alone studies, these lessons are excellent for anyone—from the beginning to the more advanced Bible student.

Prophecies of Hope are the only Bible lessons specifically written to make it easy for anyone to give Bible studies. Everything you need is included with each lesson—prophecy charts, maps, diagrams, chapter comparisons, and more! In addition, each lesson has a "looking forward" section that peaks interest for the next lesson and gives added impetus for students to continue the studies.

> *"I have concluded that the* Prophecies of Hope *lessons are the best the (Adventist) Church has. They are profound in their scope and approach. I really mean this, and I now use them and recommend them exclusively."*
> —Rick Blythe, pastor

> *"I have been using the* Prophecies of Hope *lessons for some time and find they really work well in whatever part of the country I am in. I think you have your finger on the pulse of secular minded people."*
> —Emmanuel Baek, evangelist

Available as a set of 26 lessons, or individually in packs of 50.

Pacific Press®
Publishing Association
"Where the Word is life"

Three ways to order:

1	Local	Adventist Book Center®
2	Call	1-800-765-6955
3	Shop	AdventistBookCenter.com